Living
ABUNDANTLY

BRIAN L. HARBOUR

BROADMAN PRESS
NASHVILLE, TENNESSEE

Dedicated to
Clyde Herring,
Jack Gulledge,
and my Broadman editors:
early encouragers in my writing ministry

Dewey Decimal Classification: 227.5
Subject Heading: BIBLE. N.T. EPHESIANS
   CHRISTIAN LIFE
Library of Congress Catalog Card Number: 91-39694
Printed in the United States of America

Unless otherwise stated, all Scripture quotations are from the *New American Standard Bible.* © The Lockman Foundation, 1960, 1962, 1963, 1968, 1971, 1972, 1973, 1975, 1977. Used by permission.
Scriptures marked KJV are from the *King James Version of the Bible.*
Scripture quotations from *The Amplified Bible* are from *The Amplified New Testament* ©The Lockman Foundation 1954, 1958, 1987. Used by permission.

Library of Congress Cataloging-in-Publication Data
Harbour, Brian L.
    Living abundantly / Brian L. Harbour
    p. cm. -- (Living the New Testament faith. Ephesians)
    Includes bibliographical references.
    ISBN 0-8054-1017-1
    1. Bible. N.T. Ephesians--Commentaries. 2. Christian life-
-Biblical teaching. I. Title. II. Series: Harbour, Brian L.
Living the New Testament faith. Ephesians.
BS2695.3.H37 1992
227'.507--dc20

                                                        91-39694
                                                        CIP

Preface

The wife knew she had a problem but didn't know how to deal with it. Her husband thought he had a fly in his ear, so he sat around all day long with his finger in his ear. At the breakfast table, in bed, while watching television—all the time he had his finger in his ear. Finally, she took him to a doctor. The doctor told him he saw no fly in his ear.

The man was not convinced. He continued to sit around with his finger in his ear. The wife talked to the doctor privately and they devised a plan. They would fake an operation, tell the husband the fly had been removed, and the problem would be solved. So the husband agreed to the operation. The doctor put him to sleep with a mild anesthesia. When the man awoke, the doctor informed him he had removed the fly from his ear and he was now well. The doctor stopped by to check on the man before releasing him. He found the man sitting up in bed, with a big smile on his face, and his finger in his ear! The doctor said, "What are you doing? I told you I removed the fly." The man said, "I know. You don't think I want to get another fly in there, do you?"

Some people are like that. They go through life with their finger in their ear for fear something will come into their lives. Consequently, God is not able to give to them the abundant life He wants them to experience.

The call to follow Christ is the call to abundant living. God wants to fill our lives full of His richness. We have a great inheritance to claim as children of God. As we open ourselves to Christ and walk in His way, we can begin *living abundantly*.

This is the fourth in the series of devotional commentaries on the New Testament. These are written for pastors and teachers who love God's Word and who want to prepare more effectively to communicate God's Word. I hope these volumes will be helpful to you as you carry out that awesome assignment. I would love to hear from you.

Brian L. Harbour

Other Books

Contents

1 The Abundance of the Christian Life

Ephesians 1:1-14

A rich landowner named Carl often rode around his vast estate so he could congratulate himself on his great wealth. One day, while riding around his estate on his favorite horse, he saw Hans, an old tenant farmer. Hans was sitting under a tree when Carl rode by. Hans said, "I was just thanking God for my food."

Carl protested, "If that is all I had to eat, I wouldn't feel like giving thanks."

Hans replied, "God has given me everything I need, and I am thankful for it." Then the old farmer added, "It is strange you should come by today for I had a dream last night. In my dream a voice told me, 'The richest man in the valley will die tonight.' I don't know what it means, but I thought I ought to tell you."

Carl snorted, "Dreams are nonsense," and galloped away. But he could not forget Hans's words: "The richest man in the valley will die tonight." He was obviously the richest man in the valley. So he invited his doctor to his house that evening. Carl told the doctor what Hans said.

After a thorough examination, the doctor told the wealthy landowner, "Carl, you are as strong and healthy as your horse. There is no way you are going to die tonight." Nevertheless, for assurance, the doctor stayed with Carl, and they played cards through the night. The doctor left the next morning as Carl apologized for becoming so upset over the old man's dream. At about nine o'clock, a messenger arrived at Carl's door. "What is it?" Carl demanded.

The messenger explained, "It's about old Hans. He died last night in his sleep!"[1]

The richest people in the world are not those who amass worldly fortunes or those who develop lucrative portfolios. The richest people in the world are those who through Christ tap into the abundant resources God makes available. Paul began his Ephesian Letter by boldly declaring our abundance in Christ.

The Source of Our Abundance (1:1-3)

Where do these resources come from? What is the source of our abundance?

From God

Paul pointed to God as the source of our abundance. The word "grace" *(charis)* in verse 2 summarizes the blessings of the Christian life. According to Paul, "grace [comes] . . . *from* God our Father *and* the Lord Jesus Christ" (v. 2, author's italics), and we are blessed by "the God and Father of our Lord Jesus Christ" (v. 3). The abundance of the Christian life comes from God.

How distorted at times is our picture of God. We often think of God as a tyrant who capriciously moves us around like checkers on a board. Or we picture God as a judge with a long stick to rap us on the shoulder any time we get out of line. Or we understand God to be an impersonal force to whom we cannot relate in a personal way. Or we consider God a distant proprietor who is not really concerned.

That is not the biblical picture of God. Paul picked up on the picture of God given by Jesus Himself who called God our Father. God is not a tyrant, not a judge, not an impersonal force, nor a distant supervisor. He is our Father.

God has given me the privilege of being a father. My children are certainly not perfect. At times my children disappoint me. At times I am aggravated with them. But this much is certain. I want the best for them, and I will do everything within my power to provide for them. When they hurt, I hurt. When they experience failure, I share the disappointment. When they achieve success, I share the joy. I will protect them from danger and open doors of opportunity for them. I will feed them, care for them, love them, help them, encourage them in every way I can. Why? Because I am their father.

That is the way God feels toward us. He is our Father who wants the best for us and who will consequently pour into our lives His richest blessings. Our riches as Christians do not come from our own ability or our own intellect or our own achievement. We are rich because we are the children of God and He provides for us.

Through Christ

How can we tap this wealth? How can we enjoy this abundance? Paul explained that the abundant resources of God can be ours "in Christ" (v. 3). To experience the abundant resources God makes available, we must not only be in relationship with Christ; we must also live in fellowship with Christ.

We have become a cut-flower generation. We try to maintain our life and fruitfulness, but we have cut ourselves off from our sustaining roots. We seek power without prayer. We seek dynamism without devotion. We seek abundance from God without abiding in Christ. We are like cut flowers. Yet, no matter how much we water a cut flower, no matter how ingenious our attempts to keep it fresh, eventually it is going to die because it has been cut off from its sustaining roots. In a similar way, when we cut ourselves off from our flow of power through Christ we are stifling our fruitfulness and limiting our abundance. Jesus put it like this: "As the branch cannot bear fruit of itself, unless it abides in the vine, so neither can you, unless you abide in Me" (John 15:4).

As a flower without roots, so is the Christian without a dynamic, ongoing relationship with Christ. God wants to encompass our lives with His grace. He wants to enrich our lives with His blessings. But He cannot do this when we are apart from Christ or out of fellowship with Christ, for Christ is the One through whom God's blessings are supplied. God is the source of this abundance. Christ is the supplier.

The Scope of Our Abundance (1:4-12)

What kind of blessings does God want to give us? Some would suggest God wants to bless us with every material blessing. If we have enough faith, they claim, God will make us healthy and wealthy. The only problem with this health-and-wealth gospel is that it conflicts with the overall message of the New Testament. Paul was the greatest Christian of the New Testament era. Yet, his life was marked with constant conflict and perpetual problems (see 2 Cor. 11 and 12). Jesus was the Son of God. Yet, His peace was shattered by the barbs of His critics, and His life ended on a cross. Paul did not promise the first-century Christians "health and wealth." The blessings with which God wants to endow our life are not material blessings, but spiritual blessings. Paul began his Ephesian Letter with a doxology of praise to God because He "has blessed us with every spiritual blessing" (v. 3). What are the spiritual blessings, available from God through Christ, which produce abundant living?

Renewal (1:4)

The first spiritual blessing of the Christian life is the renewal which comes through election. Paul said, "He chose us in Him" (v. 4). Before the foundations of the world were set, according to the Calvinists, God chose some individuals to be saved and other individuals to be damned, and we can do nothing about it. That is not an accurate statement of the biblical doctrine of election for it leaves out individual freedom and individual responsibility. What then does the doctrine of election mean?

The doctrine of election affirms salvation begins with God.—Salvation is not something mankind does for God. It is something mankind receives from God. God takes the initiative in the process of salvation. Jesus presented this truth in John 6:44: "No one can come to Me, unless the Father who sent Me draws him." He gave the same thrust in John 15:16: "You did not choose Me, but I chose you, and appointed you." Salvation is not something we do. It is something God does. Salvation begins with God.

The doctrine of election maintains salvation is of grace.—Paul told the Ephesians, God "chose us in Him before the foundation of the world" (v. 4). If this choosing took place before the foundation of the world, then we had nothing to do with earning it. Salvation does not depend on our goodness because we could never be good enough. The rich young ruler whom Jesus encountered followed all the Commandments. He was as good as a person can be. Nevertheless, Jesus said to him, "One thing you still lack" (Luke 18:22). Salvation is not dependent on our religiosity because religion changes us from the outside in and we need something to change us from the inside out. Nicodemus was as religious as a person can be. Yet, Jesus said to him, "Truly, truly, I say to you, unless one is born again, he cannot see the kingdom of God" (John 3:3). Salvation does not depend on our goodness or our religiosity. It depends on God's grace. Salvation is of grace.

The doctrine of election explains salvation comes through Christ.— What is the basis of election? How are we chosen? Paul said, "He [God] chose us in Him [Jesus]." The basis of our election is Jesus Christ. The Calvinists were right. God does chose who will be saved and who will not be saved. And God did make that decision before the foundations of the world. But this was not a choice made arbitrarily individual by individual. God decided to choose everyone who chooses Christ, everyone who believes in Christ, everyone who yields his life to Christ. We are elected "*in* Him"(author's italics). Jesus Christ is the basis for election.

This is why the doctrine of election does not obliterate human choice or remove human responsibility. God decided to choose everyone who is in Christ. This was not plan B for God when nothing else worked, the final alternative when other alternatives did not come through. This was God's first and only plan. He made the decision to choose those who are in Christ "before the foundation of the world" (v. 4).

Do you ever wonder if you are one of God's elect? Do you ever wonder if you are chosen by God? Here's the key. Have you received Christ as your personal Savior? Are you in Him? If so, then you are chosen by God, because Christ is the basis of election.

The doctrine of election demands salvation be followed by holy living.— God chose us, Paul said, "that we should be holy and blameless before Him" (v. 4). The word translated "holy" *(hagios)* means different. For example, a temple is holy because it is different from other buildings. A priest is holy because he is different from other men. The Sabbath Day is holy because it is different from other days. The word *holy* means Christians are to be different from other people.[2]

Christians do not seem to be different from non-Christians in today's world. We usually talk and act like non-Christians, go to the same places non-Christians go, and participate in most of the same activities in which non-Christians participate. We Christians are not very different from non-Christians. When Christians today do emphasize this difference, they usually do so in a negative, pious, self-righteous way.

Our challenge as Christians is to be different, not in a negative way but in a positive way. We are to be different in our level of forgiveness, in our positive spirit, in our attitudes, in the depth of our love, and in the strength of our commitment. We are to be different in positive ways. We were chosen to be different.

Then Paul used the word "blameless" *(amomous)*. This word was used of those sacrifices which were fit to be offered to God. The word literally means "without blemish." The word "holy" has to do with our lives as they compare to others. The word "blameless" has to do with our lives as they compare to God. God not only chose us to be different from the world. He chose us to be like Him: pure, clean, and blameless.

Election is not a doctrine to be relegated to peripheral discussion or to be avoided because of its past distortion. Election is one of the richest blessings God makes available to us "in Christ" for it provides renewal.

Relationship (1:5-6)

God not only renews us. He also brings us into a relationship with Him through the process of adoption. The idea of adoption *(huithesian)* is one of the most beautiful New Testament pictures of what God has done for us. In Christ we have "adoption as sons." In the ancient world, when a person was adopted, he had all the rights of a legitimate son in his own family, and he completely lost all rights in his old family. In the eyes of the law, an adopted son was a new person. In fact, so new was he that even all debts and obligations connected with his previous family were canceled out as if they had never existed. That is what God has done for us. He adopted us into His family forever, giving us all the rights in His family. He then canceled out all of our past and made us new persons.

Just as our election was in Christ this adoption takes place "through Jesus Christ." We were not adopted into God's family because we will make such a wonderful contribution to Him. We were not adopted because of our looks, talents, or personality. We were adopted into God's family because of our decision to believe in Jesus as our Lord and Savior.

The reason for our adoption.—Our adoption was according to "the kind intention of His will" (v. 5). The phrase "kind intention" *(eudokian)* can also be translated "good pleasure." God experiences pleasure when He adopts us. He does not do this grudgingly with a heavy heart. He does so gladly with a happy heart. It is God's desire and His will to adopt us, and when He does so, it brings Him pleasure.

The result of our adoption.—Our adoption is "to the praise of the glory of His grace, which he freely bestowed on us in the Beloved" (v. 6). Our adoption gives pleasure to God and results in praise for God. Jesus said the angels rejoice over one lost soul brought into the family of God (Luke 15:10). When a person believes in Jesus and is thus adopted into the family of God, God's name is honored. We are adopted in Christ. The result is pleasure to God and praise for God.

Release (1:7-8a)

Another aspect of our blessing in Christ is the release which comes from "redemption" and "forgiveness." *Redemption* and *forgiveness* are two of the great words of the New Testament.

Redemption.—"Redemption" *(apolutrosin)* comes from a word which means to ransom. This word was used in the slave markets of the ancient world. A slave for sale was powerless to liberate himself, because he was under an obligation he himself could never pay. When someone paid a ransom for him, the slave was released to go with his new owner. The word literally means "to purchase and set free by paying a price."

That is what God did for us. He bought us on the slave market of sin and He set us free. What was the ransom paid to free us? God redeemed us "in Him" (that is, in Christ) and the price Jesus paid was "His blood" (v. 7). This is a reference to the cross and is a reminder of a basic biblical truth: without the shedding of blood there is no redemption.

Forgiveness.—The Greek word *(aphesin)* literally means *remission.* The word can be translated *dismissed.* That is, God has dismissed our sins. They have been set aside and are no longer taken into account. Therefore, we are free. Or, the word can be translated "to carry away." This is a reference to the scapegoat used on the Day of Atonement (Lev.

16). Every year, the high priest would take a goat and transfer to that goat all the sins of the people and send the goat out into the wilderness, symbolizing the carrying away of their sins. Forgiveness means our sins have been dismissed. They have been carried away.

God does not want us to live in bondage. God wants to liberate us. God does not want us to live in guilt. God wants to forgive us. God wants us to experience release.

Revelation (1:8-9)

In addition to electing us and adopting us into His forever family and setting us free to experience the fullness of life, God also revealed something to us. The phrase which ties together verses 8 and 9 is dynamite. Paul said: "In all wisdom and insight He made known to us the mystery of His will." The word "mystery" *(musterion)* does not mean something mysterious or weird. It means a sacred secret, once hidden but now revealed to God's people. The mystery about which Paul spoke was the mystery of God's plan for mankind. God has a plan for our world, a will which He wants to carry out. This is something no course of instruction, no university curriculum, and no scientific investigation will ever discover. God had to reveal this plan to Christians.

The comprehension of this revelation.—How do we comprehend what God has revealed? God revealed His plan "in all wisdom and insight" (v. 8). The word for "wisdom" *(sophia)* refers to intellectual knowledge, knowledge of things both human and divine. The word for "insight" *(phronesei)* refers to practical knowledge, the disposition of mind which enables us to know what things need to be done and what things do not need to be done. The mystery which God revealed is comprehended through our intellect and works its way out in our practice.

The compulsion of this revelation.—How did God make this plan known to us? Paul said the revelation was made "according to His kind intention which He purposed in Him" (v. 9). The meaning is clearer if we replace the pronouns with nouns. According to [God's] kind intention which [God] purposed in [Christ]. This great mystery in the heart of God, this plan God had for our world, was revealed to us through Jesus Christ. God certainly did not have to reveal this. He was under no compulsion to do so, nor did we deserve this special revelation. It came because of God's kind intention, that is, as a result of God's grace.

The consequence of this revelation.—What does God want to accomplish? God provided this revelation "with a view to an administration suitable to the fullness of the times." The Greek word for "administration" is *oikonomia.* The *oikonomos* was the house servant, the manager of the house, the one who saw to it that the family affairs ran smoothly and uninterrupted. The consequence of God's revelation is to make known His plan for the smooth operation of the world. What is this plan? The answer is in verse 10: "the summing up of all things in Christ, things in the heavens and things upon the earth."

God is working in history to unite all things in Christ. What we see all around us now is division and separation. We see that in the world: division between Jews and Gentiles; division between the rich and the poor; division between Catholics and Protestants; division between black and white. Everywhere we look in the world we see division. What is true of the world is also true of the individual. As William Barclay put it, "Every person is a walking civil war."[3] Within us is tension between right and wrong, between honesty and deception, between the desire to serve and the desire to be served, between passion and reason.

Jesus came into the world to wipe out the divisions, to remove the tensions, to close the gaps which separate and to bring us all together as one. Isn't that a wonderful prospect? God wants to bring all people and all things together. This is another of the blessings of Christ, the revelation of God's plan for the world which He has revealed to us.

Riches (1:10-11)

Paul referred to another of our blessings as Christians: "In Him also we have obtained an inheritance" (vv. 10b-11a). An inheritance is something left to someone in a will which becomes the possession of that person when the will is probated. As Christians, we have an inheritance from God.

A man worth $20 million died and left everything to his only descendent, a young nephew. However, no one knew where the young man lived. The lawyer traced him to Colorado, but then the trail ended. So he contacted a detective agency for help. The head of the agency said, "I will put my best detective on the case. She is young, sharp, opportunistic, and aggressive. She'll find your man." Three weeks later, she contacted the detective. She said, "I've found your man." "Great," the lawyer said. "When will he be back?" She answered, "Right after the honeymoon!"

That is one way to get in on an inheritance. However, we do not have to use trickery or cunning to receive our inheritance from God. It becomes ours when we commit our lives to Christ. Nothing will prevent us from receiving our rightful inheritance for everything will be carried out "according to His purpose" (v. 11). We cannot thwart the ultimate realization of God's plan. When the world is over, and all things are summed up, God will look at all things and say, "That's just the way I wanted it to happen."

The Sign of Our Abundance (1:13-14)

How can we be sure we will receive these blessings? How can we be certain God's purpose will be fulfilled? That is the work of the Holy Spirit.

I saw a little girl one Monday morning with a mark on her hand. I asked her where the mark came from. She said, "At choir last night. When I signed up for choir, they stamped my hand so everybody would know I was a part of the choir." God gives us a mark to let everybody know we are His children. We have been "sealed in Him with the Holy Spirit of promise" (v. 13). The Holy Spirit performs a present work and a future work.

The Present Work (1:13)

In the present, the Holy Spirit seals us. Four purposes of the seal were common in the ancient world.[4]

To guarantee the genuine character of a document.—A notary public uses his seal today to guarantee the genuineness of a signature. That is what the Holy Spirit does. As He comes into our lives and lives in us, He gives evidence we are genuine Christians.

To mark ownership.—We monogram shirts today to indicate ownership. When our kids go off to college or to camp, we label their clothes to indicate ownership. That is what the Holy Spirit does. As He comes into our lives and lives in us, He marks us as belonging to Christ.

To protect against tampering or harm.—We put locks on boxes to keep people from tampering with the contents. That is what the Holy Spirit does. As He comes into our lives and lives in us, He keeps us from being tampered with by Satan. He protects us.

To indicate the transaction was completed.—Today, when we complete an agreement, we put our signature on the document. This indicates the deal has been cut. In the same way, in the ancient world, when a deal had been made, the seal indicated its completion. That is what the Holy Spirit does. As He comes into our lives and lives in us, He reminds us that our redemption is complete. The deal has been cut. We now belong to God.

The Future Work (1:14)

The presence of the Holy Spirit in our lives also points to the future God has for us, for the Holy Spirit is "a pledge of our inheritance" (1:14). The Greek word for "pledge" *(arrabon)* means the earnest money on the

purchase of something. It can mean the down payment or first install-
ment. The Holy Spirit is the down payment or earnest money which
guarantees the full payment of our inheritance in the future.

This inheritance may be a reference to our resurrection body which
will be provided for us at death, a resurrection body which is adequate
for our new existence in the life to come. Or, it may be a reference to the
place prepared for us in heaven, a place Jesus said He would prepare
specifically for us. Or, it may be a symbol of the eternal fellowship we will
have with God and with the children of God through all eternity.

The Holy Spirit does provide the assurance that we will eventually
receive our inheritance. However, the most important result of the Holy
Spirit's work in us is not to provide assurance for us but to provide praise
for God. In verses 3-6, Paul talked about the riches which are ours from
God. He concluded in verse 6: "to the praise of the glory of His grace."
Then, in verses 7-12, he talked about the riches which are ours from
Christ. He concluded in verse 12: "to the praise of His glory." Then, in
verses 13-14, he talked about the riches which are ours from the Spirit.
He concluded in verse 14: "to the praise of His glory." All God has done,
when it is brought to its completion, will bring glory and honor to Him as
our Creator and our God.

For Discussion

1. What are some of the priorities for people in today's world?

2. What can we do to maintain a close fellowship with Jesus Christ?

3. Which of the blessings mentioned by Paul in the opening verses of
Ephesians is most meaningful to you?

4. Which of these blessings does the church emphasize least today?
Why?

5. What does the Holy Spirit do for the Christian?

2 | A Prayer for Friends

Ephesians 1:15-23

Many people are confused today about prayer, about what it is and how to go about it. Like the forty-year-old single lady who prayed, "Lord, I'm not asking just for myself, but please give my mother a son-in-law." Another man prayed, "Lord, bless me and my wife, son John and his wife, we four and no more. Amen!"

A close study of the Bible will reflect that prayer at its best is not centered on self but is focused on others. For example, Abraham prayed for the cities of Sodom and Gomorrah (Gen. 18); Moses prayed for God to spare the Hebrews from the wrath of His judgment (Ex. 33); Ezra prayed for the remnant who had returned to the promised land (Ezra 10); Jesus wept over the city of Jerusalem because the people would not receive their birthright from God (Luke 13:34); and Paul constantly prayed for others (Rom. 1:9; Col. 1:9; 1 Thess. 3:10). Prayer at its best always focuses on others.

When we pray for others, what should we say? Paul gave some helpful answers to that question as he prayed for his friends at Ephesus.

Thanksgiving (1:15-16)

As the little boy said his bedtime prayer, he prayed, "God, thanks for all you've done. And keep up the good work!" Some such expression of gratitude should always be a part of the Christian's prayer. As Stuart Briscoe expressed it, "When prayer becomes a shopping list and God a cut-rate supermarket operator, something big has disappeared from our relationship with Him."[1]

Paul demonstrated the attitude of gratitude in his prayers, for thanksgiving was the foundation of Paul's prayer for the Ephesians. He said, "I too, . . . do not cease giving thanks for you, while making mention of you in my prayers" (vv. 15-16). This opening statement revealed some significant truths about Paul.

Paul Prayed

The natural impact of the sentence is that Paul was a man who was regularly involved in prayer. In this practice Paul joined the company of every great Christian in every age. I have never read about or have ever known personally any Christian in whose life God was doing special things who was not committed to prayer.

Martin Luther (1483-1546) was a man of prayer, saying on one occasion, "He that has prayed well has studied well." John Wesley (1703-1791) was a man of prayer, giving the testimony, "God does nothing but in answer to prayer." David Brainerd (1718-1747) was a man of prayer, writing in his journal, "I love to be alone in my cottage, where I can spend much time in prayer."[2] That was the secret of Paul's spiritual power. He was a man of prayer.

Do you find time to pray every day? Do you begin your day with prayer? Do you end your day with prayer? Do you thank God for your food at mealtime? We will never experience the power of God in our lives unless and until we pray.

Paul Prayed for Others

Some people focus primarily on their own needs, problems, and desires when they pray. Prayer at its best focuses on the needs of others, for it grows out of a heart of concern. In a certain church paper, a typo provided an interesting thought in the pastor's column. Instead of *take* the word *fake* was printed. This resulted in the following statement from the pastor, "Many calls come to the church each week, and we conscientiously *fake* an interest in every one of them!" Paul did not fake a concern for others. His genuine concern for others was reflected in his prayers. From the testimonies in his Epistles, it is apparent that most of Paul's prayer time was spent praying for other people.

Do you pray for others each day? Do you have a prayer list of family members and friends for whom you pray every day? Paul did not just say, "I pray." Rather, in his prayers he made mention of the Ephesians. He prayed for others.

Paul Prayed Positively for Others

Four years had passed since Paul carried out his ministry in Ephesus. Because traffic by sea was very common, Paul was kept informed about the activities in Ephesus, and all of the information was not positive. Some problems developed in the church at Ephesus. Some shortcomings existed among the Christians there. Paul would address those matters in this letter. However, he did not begin with those matters. He began with a word of thanksgiving. He did not start with criticism. He started on a positive note of encouragement. He said, "I too, . . . do not cease giving thanks for you" (v. 16).

Someone described Paul's spirit of thanksgiving like this: "There are some people who, if they ever wear thankfulness at all, wear it as you do a boutonniere—on Mother's Day or at a wedding. But not Paul! He wore gratitude as a man wears his everyday suit. Praise was woven into the fabric of his life."[3]

Some people are thankful when it is expected, when it is the proper time, when they can make a show of it, or when it benefits them, but there is no genuine gratitude for other people at the core of their being. Paul, on the other hand, exuded gratitude in every letter he wrote.

Why was Paul thankful for the Ephesian Christians? He gave thanks "having heard of the faith in the Lord Jesus which exists among you, and your love for all the saints" (v. 15). These two phrases summarize the Christian life.

The loyalty of the Ephesians.—The word "faith" describes the Ephesians's attitude toward Christ. Faith means to give one's life to Jesus Christ and to leave it there. It carries with it the idea of loyalty. So the first mark of the Christian, and of the Ephesians for which Paul was thankful, was their loyalty to Christ.

The love of the Ephesians.—The word "love" describes the Ephesians's attitude toward one another. Love means to reach out our hands to others and to meet their needs. It carries with it the idea of concern. The second mark of the Christian, and of the Ephesians for which Paul was thankful, was their love for other people.

The combination.—Paul was not saying loyalty and love individually are characteristics of the Christian life. Rather, this loyalty and love must go together. The monks of the Middle Ages in Christian history had a loyalty to Christ which caused them to separate themselves from their fellowman. The heresy hunters of the Spanish Inquisition had a loyalty to Christ which made them persecute their fellowman. The Pharisees of Jesus' day had a loyalty to God which made them contemptuous of their fellowman. In contrast, the Ephesians had a loyalty to Christ which issued in love for their fellowman. That's the kind of loyalty to Christ we need to have.[4]

One of life's most significant discoveries is to realize we cannot make it alone. A wag suggests, "Behind every successful man is a loving wife and a mother-in-law in shock." That expresses an important truth. Behind every person is a network of people who help make our achievement possible. We should never pray without making mention of these people in our prayer, expressing our deepest gratitude for what they mean to our lives.

Intercession (1:17-23)

Paul not only thanked God for the Ephesians. He also interceded for them before the Father. The word *intercession* means "a meeting." Originally, it meant bumping into someone by chance on the street. Later, it came to be used for an arranged meeting, an appointment, for the purpose of speaking to someone about another person. Intercession in prayer means we use prayer as an arranged meeting, an appointment, for the purpose of speaking to God about the needs of another person.

For what did Paul pray when he interceded for the Ephesians? He wanted the Ephesians to claim all that was rightfully theirs as Christians. As Wiersbe put it, "He does not ask God to give them what they do not have but rather prays that God will reveal to them what they already have."[5] What are these things Paul wanted for the Ephesians?

That They May Understand Christ (1:17-18a)

Paul wanted the Ephesians to receive from the Spirit a continually growing supply of wisdom and clear knowledge. The word "wisdom" *(sophias)* refers to knowledge of the deep things of God. Paul wanted the Ephesians to be led deeper and deeper into the knowledge of the eternal truths of God. The word revelation *(apokalupseos)* refers to that which is explained to us, something we could not understand on our own. So Paul wanted the Ephesians to be more and more open to the things the Holy Spirit wanted to reveal to them. Many things we cannot comprehend with our natural minds. These things come only by way of revelation. Paul prayed the Ephesians would grow in their wisdom by being open more and more to the revelation of the Spirit.

Notice the intriguing phrase with which Paul started verse 18. He wrote, "I pray that the eyes of your heart may be enlightened." In biblical understanding, the heart stood for the core and center of one's being. That is why the writer of Proverbs said, "Out of it are the issues of life" (Prov. 4:23, KJV). That is why Paul said, "I pray that the eyes of your heart may be enlightened." He wanted them to know Christ in the very core and center of their being.

How can we have that understanding of Christ?

Time.—To know Christ more fully, we must spend time with Him. When I first met my wife Jan at Baylor University, I knew at once I was going to marry her. But I wanted to know her better. How did I do it? By spending time with her. As our four children grew up, we wanted to know them in all their individual uniqueness. How did we do it? By spending time with them. Whenever I have moved to a new church, one of the greatest challenges was to develop relationships with the people. How did I do it? By spending time with them. Someone once told me, "You can never develop a relationship with God in a crowd." To know Christ more fully, we must spend time with Him.

Talk.—To know Christ more fully, we must be willing to talk with Him. As a pastor, I have been blessed with many outstanding staff members who have assisted in the ministry of the church. On most occasions, I have kept the staff already established in the church. Each one had already established his or her ministry. Yet, to accomplish what the church needed, all the staff had to work together as a team toward a common goal. How could we do that? By talking with each other. The weekly staff meetings, individual conferences, social outings together— all of these enabled us to understand one another so well that we were molded into a cohesive unit. Likewise, to know Christ more fully, we must be willing to talk to Him and listen to Him in the communion of prayer.

Think.—To know Christ more fully, we must think about Him. In Paul's admonition to the Corinthians to grow, he explained that we are transformed into the image of Christ—that is, we grow spiritually—by "beholding . . . the glory of the Lord" (2 Cor. 3:18). In other words, we understand more of Christ as we concentrate on Christ. Spiritual growth is simply a process of the redirection of our concentration, changing it from self-concentration, sex-concentration, success-concentration, past-failure-concentration, and money-concentration into Christ-concentration. To know Christ more fully, we need to concentrate totally on Him.

That They May Experience Christ (1:18b-19)

Paul's concern, however, was not just for the Ephesians's minds to be expanded but also for their lives to be enriched. He wanted them to understand and experience certain things.

The hope of Christ.—Paul wanted the Ephesians to experience "the hope of His calling" (v. 18b). Someone has said life is a grindstone. It can either grind you down or polish you up. I've seen that truth verified over and over again. A tragedy comes to one person and he falls apart. He completely loses control. The same kind of tragedy comes to another person, and he rises to the occasion and seems to be strengthened by his trial. What makes the difference? It is the hope within us.

Our hope as Christians touches every aspect of our lives. We can be hopeful about the past because through Christ our sins have been forgiven and "there is therefore now no condemnation for those who are in Christ Jesus" (Rom. 8:1). We can be hopeful about the present because we know "neither death, nor life, nor angels, nor principalities, nor things present, nor things to come, nor powers, nor height, nor depth, nor any other created thing, shall be able to separate us from the love of God, which is in Christ Jesus our Lord" (vv. 38-39). We can be hopeful about the future because we know "the sufferings of this present time are not worthy to be compared with the glory that is to be revealed to us" (Rom. 8:18).

Several years ago a fire broke out in Hong and Su Dang's house. Their third child was killed in the fire. That night, as I tried to comfort this family, Hong said to me, "Preacher, if you have a car and house and job and family but don't have Jesus, you don't have anything. But even if you lose your car, and your house burns, and your baby is taken, if you have Jesus, you still have everything." That is the hope of our calling in Christ Jesus.

The fullness of Christ.—Paul also wanted the Ephesians to experience "the riches of the glory of His inheritance" (v. 18c). Did you hear about the man who became very religious at the revival meeting each year? When the invitation was given, the man would come to the front and cry out, "Fill me, Lord, fill me full." In a few weeks, he would return to his same life-style. Then, when the next revival came around, he would go through the same routine. Finally, when he went up to the front once again and began to cry, "Fill me, Lord Jesus, fill me full," the pastor prayed, "Don't do it, Lord. He leaks!"

As I watch Christians who have no joy, who do not experience the abundance Christ wants to give, I conclude they must leak. For the Bible says Jesus not only wants to save us from something but He also wants to save us for something, and that something for which he wants to save us is a full, rich, joyful life of abundance. Paul concluded his Philippian Letter with this doxology of praise, "And my God shall supply all your needs according to His riches in glory in Christ Jesus" (Phil. 4:19). That is the fullness He wants each of us to experience.

The power of Christ.—In addition, Paul wanted the Ephesians to experience "the surpassing greatness of his power toward us who believe" (v.19a). Paul described his power in the following phrase: "These are in accordance with the working of the strength of His might which he brought about in Christ" (vv. 19b-20). *Energeian* is translated "working" and refers to power which energizes a person for an activity. *Kratous* is translated "strength" and refers to power which is exercised. *Ischous* is translated "might" and refers to inherent strength. With one word after another Paul described the power which is available to the Christian through the Holy Spirit who is within us.

One of the most intriguing stories in the Bible was about Samson. A man of great power, he lost his power because he disobeyed God. He assumed he still had his power, so when the Philistines attacked, he confronted them as he had before. This time, he could not defend himself from them. The biblical writer explains why: "But he did not know that the Lord had departed from him" (Judg. 16:20). Without the presence of the Lord, Samson did not have the power of the Lord. The power comes from God, and this power is available to us.

That They May Exalt Christ (1:20-23)

Paul wanted the Ephesians's minds to be expanded and their lives to be enriched so Jesus could be exalted in their lives as the sovereign Lord.

Jesus is sovereign over death.—Jesus died, spread-eagled on a Roman cross. He was then placed in the tomb as He descended into the darkness called death. The good news is He did not stay there. He came forth alive. Paul said, "[God] raised Him from the dead and seated Him at His right hand in the heavenly places" (v. 20). That was more than just the announcement of one individual who overcame His own death. It was the announcement that death had been defeated. Jesus won the victory over death. He took the sting out of death. He removed the terror from the grave. He defeated it. Jesus has become sovereign over death.

Many years ago I preached a sermon on death from the Christian perspective in which I pointed out the terrible impact of death but at the same time the victory over death Christ provided. I had the sermon printed and one copy was picked up by a young man named Hal who had terminal cancer. He went into the hospital shortly after that and died in a few months. His wife, Joy, shared something with me a few days after he died. She said when his friends would get upset over his impending death, he would let them read his copy of my sermon on death. What he was saying was, "Don't fall apart. Death is coming for me. We all know it. But in Christ we have the victory, for He is sovereign over death."

Jesus is sovereign over history.—After Jesus' resurrection, God "seated Him at His right hand in the heavenly places, far above all rule and authority and power and dominion, and every name that is named, not only in this age, but also in the one to come" (vv. 20b-21).

Speculation arises quite often about the events in certain parts of our world being preludes to the return of our Lord and the end of the world.

Some people even set dates about when the end will come. The truth is, we do not know when the end will come or all the details. We do know this. Whenever it happens and however it happens, at that time "The kingdoms of the world have become the kingdom of our Lord, and of His Christ, and He will reign forever and ever" (Rev. 11:15), for Jesus has been raised to the right hand of God and has been declared sovereign over history.

Jesus is sovereign over the church.—God gave Jesus "as head over all things to the church, which is His body" (vv. 22-23). Christ is the head of the church.

Two pastors were constantly harassing each other about their approach to ministry. As they finished a meeting, which featured several hot debates, one remarked as he departed, "Let's just go out and continue to do the work of the church, you in your way and I in His." When we do the work of the church our way and not His way we are not doing the work of the church, for Jesus is our head. He is sovereign. He calls the shots in the church. A church which does not follow the leadership of the Lord may be a social club or a mutual congratulation society or a discussion group but it is not the church. Jesus has been established as the head of the church and we are His body.

When we intercede for others we often pray for their problems to be removed or for their burdens to be lifted or for their lives to be made easier. How much better for us to pray for others what Paul prayed for the Ephesians—that they may understand, experience, and exalt Jesus Christ.

For Discussion

1. What elements should we include in our prayers?
2. Why must love and loyalty be kept in balance in the Christian life?
3. How can we develop a more intimate relationship with Christ?
4. Why do we not experience the spiritual power God makes available to us?
5. What does the sovereignty of Christ mean for us today?

3 | The Work of Salvation

Ephesians 2:1-10

E. Stanley Jones (1884-1973) tells about an African who, after he was converted, changed his name, calling himself "After." He explained that everything important in his life happened after he met Jesus Christ.[1] We might not have changed our names after we were saved, but the point the African convert made is also true of us. Everything important in our lives happened after we met Jesus Christ. The moment we came to know Jesus in a personal way was the most important moment in life. We refer to that experience as being saved. No passage of Scripture so clearly explains the dynamics of the experience of salvation as the opening verses of Ephesians. Paul made a powerful presentation about the work of salvation.

The Work Against God (2:1-3)

Before we can understand the work of God for us we need to understand our work against God. Instead of living in fellowship with God, we chose to move away from God. Instead of obeying God, we chose to disobey God. This moving away from God and this disobedience of God brought spiritual death.

A little girl about eight wrote a letter to God as a part of a special project in Sunday School. The letter said, "Dear God, what is it like to die? Signed, Sue." Then she added, "P.S., I just want to know. I don't want to do it." No one wants to die, and many die before they are ready. Nevertheless, physical death is a reality for all of us. The real tragedy, however, is not the death a person experiences at the end of his life but the death that comes while he is still living. Not physical death but spiritual death, not the separation of the soul from the body but the separation of the soul from God—that is the real tragedy.

Paul described this spiritual death in the opening verses of chapter 2. A person is not physically dead without Christ. He still breathes, talks, and carries on his life. A person is not intellectually dead without Christ. He still thinks and reasons about some things. A person is not morally dead without Christ. People without Christ do at times exhibit kindness and display love. Paul was talking about a spiritual condition, about spiritual death, a death which is experienced in the midst of physical life. Paul expressed the same truth in 1 Timothy 5:6: "But she who gives herself to wanton pleasure is dead even while she lives."

The Cause of Spiritual Death (2:1)

How does this spiritual death occur? Paul mentioned two causal factors in spiritual death: "trespasses and sins." Trespasses refers to deviations from the straight and narrow path. The Greek word *(paraptomasin)* means to lose your way or to go astray. "Sins" refers to missing the mark with our life. The Greek word *(hamartiais)* means to shoot an arrow at something and miss the target.

These two words present the heart of the New Testament concept of sin. To sin means to deviate from the pathway God wants us to follow and to fall short of the goal God wants us to reach. Sin means to be less than what God wants us to be and to end up in a place where God does not want us to go. The result of this deviation from God's plan is spiritual death.

The Condition of Spiritual Death (2:1)

When is a person dead physically? Surprisingly, no unanimity can be found on that question. Some say a person is dead when the heart stops functioning. With the development of the heart-lung machine, this definition is inadequate. This machine is able to keep the blood flowing and the vital signs functioning artificially, and thus keeps a person alive even after his heart stopped functioning. Therefore, a person is not necessarily dead when his heart has stopped functioning.

Others define death on the basis of a nonfunctioning brain, a condition determined by a series of tests including an EEG, a check of responses to external stimuli, and a test of the central nervous system. In other words, when the brain stops functioning, a person is dead. This is the generally accepted definition today, and I believe it gives some striking parallels to the matter of spiritual death.

Spiritual death means the inability to reason about spiritual matters.— When I was in high school we always dreaded the first week of basketball practice. We'd spend those first days getting our legs in shape. We would go up and down the bleachers. We would run back and forth between the lines on the court. We would do this until we all dropped in our tracks. After the first day our feet, covered with blisters, were so sensitive we could hardly touch them. Each day we would put a layer of this gooey mess called "toughskin" on our feet. Within a week, our blisters had turned to callouses so thick and hard I could stick a pin straight into them and not even feel it. They had become hardened. No longer were my feet sensitive to pain.

That is what sin does to our lives. When we first commit a sin, it pricks our conscience. We know it is wrong, and it hurts. However, the more we commit sin, the less we feel it, and before we know it our soul has become so calloused, our conscience so confused, we no longer can discern between right and wrong. Our spiritual reasoning power has ceased to function. We are spiritually dead.

"This is the way of an adulterous woman," the writer of Proverbs said, "She eats and wipes her mouth, and says, 'I have done no wrong' " (30:20). When a person can no longer discern between right and wrong, when one can sin and no longer feel it, one is spiritually dead.

Spiritual death means the inability to respond to spiritual stimuli.—As physical death is marked by the inability to respond to external stimuli, spiritual death is marked by the failure to respond to external stimuli. Put a live person at an exciting football game, send him to a stimulating movie, give him a dramatic book, expose him to a matchless sunset, and he goes crazy. Put a dead person in the same places, expose him to the same things, and what does he do? Nothing! Because, being dead, he is no longer able to respond to external stimuli. That is a sign of his deadness.

Put a person who is spiritually alive in an exciting worship service, give him an opportunity to share his faith, expose him to a need he can meet in Christ, let him have an hour with his Bible, and he'll go crazy. Put a spiritually dead person in the same places, give him the same opportunities, and what does he do? Nothing! He is bored. Why? Because, being spiritually dead, he is no longer able to respond to external stimuli. That is a sign of his spiritual deadness.

A person is spiritually dead when he can no longer reason about spiritual matters and when he can no longer respond to spiritual stimuli.

The Contributors to Spiritual Death (2:2-3)

Paul pointed to three forces which contribute to our spiritual condition: the world, the devil, and the flesh.

The world.—We often allow ourselves to be controlled by the values and attitudes of the world. John, in his First Epistle, described the value system of the world in three phrases: "the lust of the flesh and the lust of the eyes and the boastful pride of life" (1 John 2:16). When we live with trespasses and sins we are not living the way a Christian lives but rather we are living the way the world lives.

The devil.—We yield to the devil and let him control our lives. Peter, in his First Epistle, described the devil as "a roaring lion, seeking someone to devour" (1 Pet. 5:8). When we live with trespasses and sins we are not living under the control of Christ but rather we are living under the control of Satan whom Paul called "the prince of the power of the air" (v. 2).

The flesh.—We follow the desires of the flesh. By desire *(epithumiais)* Paul meant the desire for the wrong and forbidden thing. By flesh *(sarkos)* Paul did not mean one's body but one's sin nature within (v. 3). When we live with trespasses and sins we are not displaying the spirit of obedience which comes from the Spirit but rather we are displaying a spirit of disobedience which comes from the flesh.

What is the conclusion? Notice what Paul said in the final phrase of verse 3. He told the Ephesians they were by nature children of wrath. The word for wrath *(orge)* does not describe an explosive burst of anger but rather a settled indignation. Instead of being children of God who experience His love we are children of wrath who experience His settled indignation. The work against God results in spiritual death.

The Work of God (2:4-9)

In verse 4, Paul made a transition, and what a wonderful transition it is. In this passage, Paul answered some of the most important questions about God's work of redemption through Christ Jesus.

What? (2:5)

Paul began with a declaration of what God did. God "made us alive together with Christ and raised us up with Him" (2:5). In the New Testament, three different Greek words are translated "life." *Bios*, from which we derive the word *biology*, refers to the physical life of bone and flesh we have in common with animals. *Psuche*, from which we get our word *psychology*, means soul. In its New Testament usage, the word does not refer to a person's soul in contrast to his body. Rather, the *psuche* is the whole human person, the person who is more than just physical, the person who has a spiritual capacity. *Zoe*, from which we get our word *zoology*, is abundant life. It is full or whole life. It is the extra additive that puts zest in life.

Paul used the third word in our text. When God made us alive together with Christ, He gave us *zoe*. We already have *bios*: life force. We already have *psuche*: a spiritual capacity. Only from God, as His gift, can we have *zoe*—whole life. Life, real life, comes only from God. In Christ, God gives us life.

When? (2:5)

When did God do this for us? God provided this life "even when we were dead in our transgressions" (v. 5). God took care of this matter when we did not deserve it, when nothing attractive in our lives would call forth this kind of response from Him.

A young man, in love for the first time, was trying to impress his girlfriend. So he bought a dozen roses and knocked on her door, the roses behind his back. When she opened the door, he shoved the roses at her and smiled. She was so excited she grabbed him and began to kiss him. He broke loose, dropped the roses, and ran away. "Don't leave," she said, "I didn't mean to scare you." "You didn't scare me," the young man responded. "I'm just going to get some more roses!"

We do not have to bring any roses to God to induce Him to love us. Before we were worthy of His attention, while still dead in our trespasses and sin, through Christ, God established a way in which we could be made alive together with Him.

Why? (2:5)

Why did God do this for us? Paul explained His motive. God did this "because of His great love with which He loved us" (v. 4). We have heard this truth and sung this truth for so long the incredible impact of it is often missed. God loves us. Let that phrase rumble through your mind for a little while. The omnipotent Creator of the world loves us. The holy God of Israel loves us. The sovereign Father of the Son of God loves us. That is the good news we must never tire of proclaiming.

A little girl wrote to her pastor one day: "Dear Pastor, I know God loves me but I wish He would give me an A on my report card so I could know for sure!" God did something even better to prove His love. He sent Jesus to the cross to show us there was no line beyond which His love would not go. From the moment of creation to the moment of consummation, God is driven by the motive of love.

How? (2:5)

Paul said God "made us alive together with Christ" (v. 5). This new life we experience as Christians was made possible because of Christ. In His virtuous life and His vicarious sacrifice on the cross, Jesus paid the penalty for our sin. He thus made it possible for God to forgive us and restore us to a right relationship with Him. Paul's statement in 1 Corinthians 5:21 is as clear an explanation of this process as is found in the New Testament. "He made Him who knew no sin to be sin on our behalf, that we might become the righteousness of God in Him." The one word which summarizes this process is the word *grace*. Paul introduced the word in verse 5. He elaborated on it in verses 8-9.

For What? (2:6-7)

What is the result of this transformation God accomplished for us? We see the present result in verse 6. We see the future result in verse 7.

Look at verse 6. God "raised us up with Him, and seated us with Him in the heavenly places, in Christ Jesus." This is present tense. This is what we are already experiencing right now. Just as we have already been raised up with Jesus, even so we are already seated with Him in the heavenly places. What does that mean? It means our names are already inscribed in heaven's register. It means our interests are already being promoted there. It means the blessings of heaven are already descending on us. Right now, we are already enjoying the power and the position of being children of God.

But there is more. Look at verse 7. God did His work of redemption in us "in order that in the ages to come He might show the surpassing riches of His grace in kindness toward us in Christ Jesus." Suppose we were left an inheritance of a billion dollars from which we could draw we wanted anytime we wanted. Think how foolish we would be if we drew something out initially, but then never touched the inheritance anymore. Potentially rich, we would be living in poverty.

This is the spiritual picture Paul gave in verse 7. We have been left an inheritance. He called it "the surpassing riches of God's grace." It is so vast we cannot even put a value on it, so limitless it is inexhaustible. However, so many Christians, after having made their initial withdrawal at the point of conversion, have never touched the inheritance since then. Potentially rich, they are living in spiritual poverty.

God's purpose for us is not just past but also present, not just for our conversion but for our completion, not just to save us from our sin but to fill out life full.

For How Long? (2:8-9)

Ray Summers refers to the phrase "by grace you have been saved," which appears in verses 5 and 8, as "one of the most meaningful grammatical constructions in the New Testament." It is a perfect passive participle. The perfect tense describes an action which is a state of being. Paul said, "By grace we are in the state of being of having been saved." This state of being is continuous in the absolute sense. Summers concludes, "This speaks with assurance of the security of that one who has been given spiritual life in association with Christ. He is in a state of having been saved so that he can never die spiritually again."[2]

When Jesus saves us, we are saved for good. How can we experience this permanent salvation? Notice the two key phrases: "by grace" and "through faith."

By grace.—This is God's part in the transaction. Grace has been described as "God's riches at Christ's expense." Grace is the unmerited favor of God. The word *grace* describes God's willingness to love us when we were unlovely and to offer us the gift of life.

Through faith.—This is our part in the transaction. Faith is a process that involves both the mind and the will. Faith means to believe with our mind this gift is available through Christ. Faith also means to decide with the will we want this gift and are willing to let Christ take control of our lives.

Grace comes first, and then faith responds to it. Grace is what God does. Faith is our response to what God has done. We are saved "by grace" and "through faith." The wonderful work of God is the work of salvation.

The Work for God (2:10)

God not only saves us from something. He saves us for something. Paul expressed that truth is an intriguing way in verse 10 when he wrote"We are His workmanship, created in Christ Jesus for good works." The Greek word is *poiema.* We get our word *poem* from that word. We are God's poem. What does it mean to be God's poem?

Originality

A poem is a creative piece of originality. My first experience at writing was composing lyrics for songs. Here are some of the most outstanding titles: "I Love You with All My Heart," "The Beauty of a Girl in Love," and "I've Got That Brokenhearted Feeling Again." If you can say anything about my songs—and you can't say much—it is that they were original. That is the nature of poetry. No two poems are exactly alike. Their rhythm is different. Their meter is different. Their rhyming is different. They are different. A poem is a creative piece of originality. And Paul said we are God's poem. We need to learn that about ourselves. God did not make us like anyone else. He made us unique. He made us different.

When Marlo Thomas began her acting career her famous actor father gave her a bit of advice. He said, "Marlo, just remember, you are a thoroughbred, and thoroughbreds don't watch other horses. They just run

their own race."[3] Through Christ we have been created into thoroughbreds. We are not to watch other Christians but are to run our own race.
We are each a creative piece of God's originality.

Identity

Even though all poems are original and unique, each poem by a writer
has a mark on it that identifies it with him. The author has a certain style,
a certain theme, perhaps some key words, which repeatedly appear. Although each poem is unique, a thread of similarity identifies them with
the one who wrote them.

As you live out the creativity God has planted within you, do you do it
in a way that calls attention to the fact that you belong to God? Do you
have God's stamp upon your life? An anonymous poet expressed this
truth beautifully:

> Big Sam was humble and quiet,
> And very slow of speech.
> But he touched the hearts of several
> His pastor couldn't reach,
> Because he lived the sermon
> He knew he could't preach.

Is that true of you? We are not just a poem. We are God's poem. As we
live out our lives, something about us should let people know we belong
to God.

Purpose

A poem also has a purpose. A person does not write a poem just to
express creative originality. A person does not write a poem just to have
something to identify with them. A poem has a purpose. A person writes
a poem to accomplish something, to communicate a message. So it is
with God's poems. "We are His workmanship," Paul said, "created in
Christ Jesus for good works" (v. 10). God did His re-creative work in us
for a reason, and Jesus explained that reason in His Sermon on the
Mount when He said, "Let your light shine before men in such a way that
they may see your good works, and glorify your Father who is in heaven"
(Matt. 5:16).

We spend so much time saying, "Works cannot save a person" that we
forget this other very clear message of the New Testament: a saved person should be involved in works (2 Cor. 9:8; Col. 1:10; 2 Tim. 3:17; Titus
2:14). Our purpose is to do the work of God. We are to be busy for Him.

Lloyd C. Douglas (1877-1951) was an outstanding preacher-writer of
another generation. He authored *Magnificent Obsession* and *The Robe*,

among others. His first published work was titled *More Than a Prophet*. The book did not sell well. Of the copies which sold, Douglas bought half of them himself. He always joked that *More Than a Prophet* was less than a profit.[4]

Every Christian is a published work of God. If we will remember our uniqueness, reflect our identity with Him, and be busy about the work He has given us to do, then we can be more than a profit to Him.

For Discussion

1. What does it mean to sin?
2. What are the characteristics of spiritual death?
3. Contrast what we do to ourselves by our sin with what God wants to do for us by salvation?
4. What is grace? What is faith? How are the two related?
5. What works can we do to demonstrate our relationship with God?

4 | United in Christ

Ephesians 2:11-22

When Linus was watching television, Lucy entered the room and told him to change channels. Linus asked, "What makes you think you can walk right in here and take over?" Lucy doubled up her fist and snarled, "These five fingers. Individually they're nothing but when I curl them together like this into a single unit, they form a weapon that is terrible to behold." Without another word, Linus responded, "Which channel do you want?" Turning away, he looked at his fingers and inquired, "Why can't you guys get organized like that?"[1]

Paul told the Ephesians that God wanted to bring all Christians together in a unity which will enable us to do together what we could never have done alone. That theme of unity, which permeates the entire Ephesian Epistle, is the special focus of this section.

Removed from Christ (2:11-12)

A certain glamour is attached to the life-style of the world, and those who follow this life-style have a certain condescension toward those who are involved in religion. Those who follow the playboy philosophy, those who grab for all the gusto they can find, those who promote personal pleasure as their primary purpose, those who live secular lives in complete neglect of God claim to be the "with-it" people of our day. They communicate to those who identify with Christ that we are missing out on what life is really like. We Christians hear the message so often we are at times tempted to believe it.

It reminds me of the old rooster with his chickens. Some boys were playing football nearby and accidentally kicked the football into the chicken yard. The rooster saw the football, thought about the eggs his hens were laying, and said, "I don't want to be too critical, Girls, but I want you to look at what size eggs they are putting out on the other side of the fence!" Before we long too much for what is happening out in the world, we need to hear how Paul described those who are in the world.

34

He said the person in the world is not "with it" but instead he is "without."

Without Christ (2:12)

The Smith family experienced every parent's nightmare. Turning the corner in their car the back door came open. Jimmy, five years old, was leaning against the door. Somehow he managed to hold onto the armrest and window handle until the father stopped the car, and he was not injured. That night, as the mother put Jimmy to bed, she said, "Jimmy, we need to thank Jesus for saving you today." Little Jimmy responded, "Why should we thank Jesus? I'm the one who held on!"

Closer to the truth is the statement one of my church members made one time. After the funeral of a dear man in our church, his wife told me, "I just couldn't make it without Jesus." Yet, that is exactly what the person of the world has to do. The person in the world is "separate from Christ" (v. 12). He has to try to make it in life without Christ: without Christ to share his burdens, without Christ to forgive his sins, without Christ to show him God's way, without Christ to go with him into the dark shadows of death.

Without Citizenship (2:12)

The person in the world is also without citizenship. Paul described him as being "excluded from the commonwealth of Israel" (v. 12). Paul was probably speaking figuratively here. By "Israel" he had in mind the new work of God through Christ. He was talking about the kingdom of God. Two kingdoms exist in the world today. These two kingdoms—the kingdom of this world and the kingdom of God—operate side by side. We have to choose to be in one or the other. Jesus is the door by which a person moves from the kingdom of this world into the kingdom of God. When we accept Him, we become a part of God's kingdom. When we reject Him, we are a part of the world's kingdom. Our response to Christ is the key.

This is important because someday everything around us will be gone. The kingdoms of this world will be swallowed up in the kingdom of God and His Christ, for only the kingdom of God is eternal. When a person is without Christ he is without citizenship in the only kingdom that is eternal.

Without Covenants (2:12)

The person in the world is also without covenants. The word *covenant* is one of the most important words in the Bible. It describes a relationship with God in which He makes certain promises to us. The Bible is a book of promises. Someone estimated there are 30,000 promises in the Bible. That number probably evolved from the fact there are 31,173 verses in the Bible and from the assumption every verse contains a promise. Another man actually counted 7,487 specific promises by God to mankind in the Bible.

I don't know how many promises the Bible contains, but I do know this. Every one of them is for those who have a relationship with God through Christ. In contrast, the person in the world is not only without Christ and without citizenship in the only eternal kingdom, he is always without the benefit of the promises of God.

Without Confidence (2:12)

The person of the world is also without "hope and without God in the world." The confidence sometimes displayed by those in the world is a false confidence for it has no deep roots or solid foundation. Confidence is not based on our own strength and our own ability. Confidence is based on the presence of God in us, the provisions of God for us, and the promises of God to us. Hope is based on the knowledge of God's promises and the confidence that He will make good on those promises. As William Hendriksen put it, hope is "the conviction that all things will be well, even when all things seem to be wrong."[2] The person in the world does not have confidence because he does not have a connection with God. The Gentiles had gods. The pagan world of Paul's day worshiped a proliferation of gods. But they were without the one true God. They did not know the true God and therefore did not experience the peace, power, and purity which is available only through Him.

Paul's discussion in verses 11-12 was directed specifically at the Gentiles, those who were "called 'Uncircumcision' by the so-called 'Circumcision' " (v. 11). However, it is applicable to everyone who stands apart from Christ. But here is the good news. God wants to gather to Himself all who are apart from Him and create a new unity. How can that be done?

Reconciled to Christ (2:13)

Throughout the Bible, terminology of distance was used to distinguish between Jews and Gentiles. Those who were a part of the covenant with Israel were nearby. Those who were not a part of the covenant with Israel were far away. Isaiah spoke of "peace to him who is far off and to him who is near" (Isa. 57:19). In Peter's Pentecost sermon, he said, "The promise is for you and your children, and for all who are far off" (Acts

2:39). Gentiles were far off and Jews were nearby. However, Jesus changed that. Now in Christ Jesus those who formerly were far off have been brought near.

"Now," in verse 13, stands in stark contrast to "at that time" in verse 12. In the past, Jews were nearby because the blood of Abraham flowed in their veins. Now, Paul explained, the ones who were nearby were those for whom Jesus had shed His blood. It is not the blood in our veins but the blood shed for us on the cross that determines whether we are nearby or faraway. Jews as well as Gentiles could be faraway if they rejected Christ. Gentiles as well as Jews could be nearby if they received Christ. Reconciliation comes not because of who we are or what we have. Reconciliation comes through Christ. This change in our relationship with God also changes our relationship with one another.

Related in Christ (2:14-18)

Who are the two groups referred to in verse 14? This is a reference to the Jews and the Gentiles. These were the two groups God wanted to bring together in Christ. In order to accomplish this unification, God had to break down some barriers.

The Barriers (2:14-15a)

Between these two groups was "the barrier of the dividing wall" (v. 14). The barrier between the Jews and the Gentiles was formally symbolized by two things.

The barrier in the temple.—The court of the Gentiles was separated from the temple proper by a wall or barrier. On this barrier was an inscription which said: "Let no one of another nation come within the fence and barrier around the Holy Place. Whoever will be taken doing so will himself be responsible for the fact that his death will ensue."[3] That barrier in the temple formed a dividing wall between Jews and Gentiles.

The barrier of the law.—Another dividing wall between Jews and Gentiles was the law with its requirements. The moral emphasis of the law was deemphasized as the ceremonial emphasis was magnified. The rules and regulations which evolved from the law formed a dividing wall between Jew and Gentile. Because the Gentiles did not follow all the regulations and restrictions of the oral tradition developed from the law, they were considered to be separated from God.

The Blessing (2:15b-16)

What did Jesus do for these two groups? The phrase in verse 15 is an interesting one. Jesus made "the two into one new man." The Greeks had two words which could be translated new: *neos* which means new in point of time and *kainos* which means a new thing which did not exist before. Paul used the word *kainos* in this fifteenth verse. Jesus brought together the Jews and Gentiles and from the both produced one new kind of person.[4] Jesus did not simply bring the Jews and Gentiles together. He brought them together in such a way that they became an altogether new creature.

How did Jesus do that? How did He break down the barrier between Jew and Gentile and make them one? Jesus brought the Jew and Gentile together by abolishing in His flesh the enmity caused by the law of God (v. 15). The law of God does not save anyone. The law of God simply reminds us of our sins. The law reminds us therefore of the enmity with God caused by our sin. Jesus abolished the enmity caused by the law.

How did He do it? He did it "in His flesh" (v. 15). This is a reference to His virtuous life and His vicarious death. When Jesus lived a perfect life, He fulfilled the laws of God which mankind could never fulfill; and He exposed the laws of the Jews which mankind was never expected to fulfill. When Jesus Christ died on the cross for our sins, He removed the judgment of the law and the enmity which it caused. All of us now are in one group, for both Jew and Gentile have been redeemed through the cross and ushered into the family of God. Therefore, there is no longer any difference between Jew and Gentile in the eyes of God. The difference is between those who are in Christ and those who are not in Christ.

The Benefit (2:17-18)

Because of what Jesus did on the cross, we have two things: peace and access.

Peace.—In verse 17, Paul said, "And He came and preached peace to you who were far away, and peace to those who were near." Peace *(eirenen)* is the inner assurance that all is right between us and God. Notice the relationship of Christ to our peace. "For He Himself is our peace, . . . thus establishing peace" (vv. 14-15). "He . . . preached peace to you" (v. 17). Jesus' entire life was a mission of peace.

Access.—In verse 18, Paul said, "For through Him we both have our access in one Spirit to the Father." Access is the freedom to approach God because of the confidence that we have found favor with Him. The Greek word translated "access" *(prosagogen)* was used in a number of ways in the ancient world. It was used for bringing men into the presence of God so they could be consecrated to His service. It was used for introducing a speaker or an ambassador into the national assembly. It was used for ushering a person into the presence of a king. Through Christ, we have been given access to God who provides peace within, a peace which derives from the knowledge we are accepted by God.

Restructured by Christ (2:19-22)

Jesus took the two groups, Jews and Gentiles, and made them into a new group in which all of the previous distinctions were no longer important. He broke down the barriers between them. That produced a changed status for these Gentiles, and Paul talked about that in verse 19: "So then you are no longer strangers and aliens."

Paul described the Gentiles with two words: "strangers and aliens." The word "strangers" *(xenoi)* means foreigners, someone from another place, and in the ancient world the foreigner was always regarded with suspicion and dislike. The word translated "alien" *(paroikoi)* was a resident alien. He lived in the city, but had never become a naturalized citizen. He even paid a tax for the privilege of existing in a land which was not his own. But the alien was never included in things. He always lived on the edge.[5]

Paul said to the Gentiles, "That's the way you were. You were looked at with suspicion and dislike by God's people. Even for those of you who were drawn to Israel's God, you were always on the edge." Paul added, "Now your status has changed. In the New Israel, which is the church, you are no longer regarded with suspicion. You are no longer on the edge"(author's words).

God has restructured the world through Christ. This restructuring allows every person, Jew and Gentile alike, to participate in three new entities.

Citizens of the Kingdom (2:19)

Paul described the Gentiles as "fellow-citizens with the saints" (v. 19). This is the only place in the New Testament where the word translated "fellow-citizens" is found, and it suggests equality in all ways. The terms of admission to the kingdom of God are the same for the Gentile as for the Jew. A person must simply believe to become a part of the kingdom of God, believe and nothing more. The standing in the kingdom of God is the same for the Gentile as for the Jew. The church is not divided into first-class Christians and second-class Christians. We are all in the same class. The privileges extended to those in the kingdom of God are the same for the Gentile as for the Jew. Some in the kingdom do not have more privileges than others.

Believers from Israel and believers from outside of Israel have been brought together into one new kingdom called the kingdom of God in which everyone has the same requirements, the same standing, and the same privileges.

Members of the Family (2:19)

A home is a more intimate unit than a nation. Paul used the home to describe the new people of God formed by Jesus Christ. Through Christ, Jews and Gentiles alike become a part of "God's household" (v. 19).

This image goes beyond the image of Christians as citizens of the kingdom. To be fellow citizens with someone else expresses some commonality. But to be brothers and sisters takes that relationship to a new level of intimacy. The New Testament not only talks about the kingdom of God. It also talks about the family of God. Kingdom of God pictures individuals who are willing to relate to one another. Family of God pictures individuals who are related to one another by blood. We do not sing today, "I'm so glad I'm a part of the kingdom of God." We sing that we are glad we are a part of the "family" of God.

Believers from Israel and believers from outside of Israel have been brought together into one new family in which we are all intimately related to one another.

Bricks in God's Building (2:20-22)

Paul presented yet another image of the church. He spoke of the church as a building. This is a very helpful analogy because we all know how a house is built. We start with a good foundation. Then, we follow the plan for constructing the building correctly, using good material as we put it together. The church is put together in this same fashion.

The foundation of this building (v. 20).—This building is "built upon the foundation of the apostles and prophets, Christ Jesus Himself being the corner stone" (v. 20). Paul said in 1 Corinthians 3:11 that "no man can lay a foundation other than the one which is laid, which is Jesus Christ." Paul's statement here was not contradictory. He just used a little different imagery. Here, Paul spoke of the apostles and prophets as the foundation and Christ Jesus as the cornerstone.

The word apostle means "one who is sent under the authority of another." The word became a technical term to identify the twelve who were first chosen to follow Jesus. It is probably the technical meaning of the term Paul had in mind here. As the first twelve followers of Jesus, the apostles were foundational in building the church.

When Paul mentioned prophets we immediately think about the Old Testament men like Elijah, Elisha, Jeremiah, and Isaiah. However, Paul was probably not referring to the Old Testament prophets. We conclude that for several reasons. Paul mentioned the apostles first and then the prophets. He would probably have spoken of the prophets first if he had the Old Testament characters in mind because they came chronologically before the apostles. In Ephesians 4:8-11 the prophets are mentioned immediately after the apostles. These prophets were gifted by the ascended Lord and thus must be someone in the New Testament area. In Ephesians 3:5, "apostles and prophets" appears in that order, and the reference here clearly excluded prophets of the old covenant.

Who then were these prophets? The prophets of the New Testament were those who spoke forth the Word of God. So the foundation of the church was not only the apostles, those men who first demonstrated the faith to follow Jesus. The foundation of the church was also the prophets, those who faithfully proclaimed God's Word.

These two—apostles and prophets—were foundational only in the secondary sense. Jesus was the primary foundation, and that is why Paul referred to Him as the cornerstone. The cornerstone of the building finalizes the shape of the building and thus determines the lay of its walls. All the other stones of a building are adjusted to the cornerstone. We are the living stones with which Jesus builds His church. The foundation of the church is comprised of those who in faith follow Jesus and those who in boldness proclaim the message about Him. Jesus holds a strategic spot in the building of the church. He is the cornerstone.

The function of this building (vv. 20-21).—Paul reminded the Ephesians that the desire of Christ is for His church to grow. The church is not to be static. We are not just to hold our own. We are not merely to settle into the status quo. We are to grow, numerically and spiritually.

In addition, Paul reminded the Ephesians that each one of us can and should make a contribution to that growth. He said the building is "being fitted together" (v. 21). The picture is of separate stones which one by one are put in place as the building is constructed, each stone important and essential. In the same way, each of us can make a significant contribution to the growth of the church.

Further, Paul reminded the Ephesians the goal of growth is that the church might become holy. God wants us to grow into a "holy temple." Holy does not mean perfect. It means cleansed and consecrated for the task God wants us to carry out.

Finally, Paul reminded the Ephesians this growth is only possible in relationship with Jesus Christ. This growth toward holiness, Paul said, will take place "in the Lord" (v. 21). In vital union with Him, the church will experience growth. In vital union with Him, each individual Christian can make a significant contribution. In vital union with Him, we can become holy.

The future of this building (v. 22).—Paul elaborated further on the idea of the church as a building. Paul described the church with the symbols of a nation, a family, and a building. He told the Ephesians that those individuals and churches who live in vital union with Christ will grow. To help the Gentiles in Ephesus realize they were included in this process, Paul said, "You also are being built together in a dwelling of God." He wanted the Gentiles to be aware they were not left out. They were not excluded. They were a part of this grand work God was doing in building His church. They too could experience the growth Paul described. They could also be a part of the growth in unity which Paul declared.

How could they grow in unity? Paul said it occurred "in the Spirit" (v. 22). The unity of the church does not come from our organization, our style of worship, or our denominational name. The unity of the church comes from the Spirit of God at work in and through Jesus Christ. When we become organized around Christ, we will be an army for God's kingdom which is awesome to behold.

For Discussion

1. What are some of the things a Christian has that a non-Christian does not have?

2. What groups, like the Gentiles in the first century, are we excluding today from the offer of reconciliation?

3. What barriers keep unbelievers away from the church?

4. What image most clearly describes the church: the picture of a nation, of a family, or of a building?

5. How can we enhance unity among Christians today?

5 | A Portrait of Paul

Ephesians 3:1-13

Have you ever heard of Annie Taylor? She was a forty-three-year-old schoolteacher from Bay City, Michigan, who wanted to be rich and famous. Widowed and childless, she was a woman looking for a cause to which she could give herself. She decided to be the first person to ride in a barrel over Niagara Falls.

Nearby Buffalo hosted the Pan-American Exposition in October, 1901, an event which would draw large crowds to the Niagara Falls area. Annie Taylor hired an agent to promote her stunt, and thousands of spectators came to see this middle-aged schoolteacher who couldn't even swim go over the falls. In a barrel four-and-a-half feet high, weighing 160 pounds, Annie did what no one had ever done before and survived with only minor injuries. As soon as she recovered from the stunt, she began a lecture tour. Unfortunately, her presentation was boring and soon no one attended her lectures. She returned to Niagara Falls, broke. When she died twenty years later she gave this testimony, "I did what no other woman in the world had nerve enough to do, only to die a pauper."[1]

Riches escaped Annie Taylor, not because she lacked courage and commitment, but because of her motive and resulting goals. Driven by desire for personal glory, she gave herself to a trivial cause.

How different from Paul. Two thousand years after Paul lived, men and women the world over look to him for spiritual direction and insight. His letters are studied throughout the world. His life is held up as an example of commitment. Why the difference between Paul and Annie Taylor? Annie Taylor was driven by a desire for self-glory; Paul was driven by a desire to glorify God. Annie Taylor gave herself to a trivial cause; Paul gave himself to a preeminent cause.

The dynamics of Paul's life of faith are evident in this Ephesian Letter as he explained the message, motive, and meaning of his life.

The Renunciation Demonstrated by Paul (3:1)

Linus and Charlie Brown were talking one day. Said Linus, "When I grow up, I'm going to be a real fanatic." Charlie Brown asked, "What are you going to be fanatical about, Linus?" With a quizzical look Linus responded, "Oh, I don't know. It doesn't really matter. I'll be sort of a wishy-washy fanatic."[2] There was nothing wish-washy about Paul. In fact, the most remarkable thing about his life was his willingness to stand up for his convictions. Sometimes it cost him. That's why Paul referred to himself as a "prisoner of Christ Jesus for the sake of you Gentiles" (v. 1). Paul was in fact in prison at Rome when he wrote this epistle. However, Paul did not consider himself to be a prisoner of Rome. He considered himself a prisoner of Christ because he had been arrested in Christ's service. Paul would not compromise his convictions, not even if it cost him his freedom. He was willing to sacrifice for what He believed.

I'm afraid we have lost that element of sacrifice today. At crunch time, instead of opting for what is right, we usually take the popular pathway. Instead of being moved by conviction, we usually yield to convenience.

Patrick (ca. 390-461), the patron saint of the Irish, was still preaching and carrying out his ministry at an advanced age. He led a pagan king to faith in Christ and was to baptize him. Early the next morning, Saint Patrick led the convert into the river. Patrick took an iron standard formed as a cross into the water to indicate the chieftain was being baptized in the name of Christ. Because of poor eyesight, Saint Patrick thrust the sharpened point of the standard through the foot of the baptismal candidate! Only when the blood came to the water's surface did the saintly preacher realize what he had done. With great sorrow, he asked the young man, "My Son, why did you not cry out?" The new convert responded, "Why should I cry out, Father? I thought it was part of the baptism!"[3]

We need to realize again today that the call to sacrifice is a part of the baptism! No cheap crosses are available. No easy road is acceptable. Christ calls us to take up our cross and follow Him (Mark 8:34). Christ does not call us to be prima donnas but prisoners.

We cannot understand Paul unless we recognize the depth of his commitment to Christ. Because Jesus was in charge of Paul's life, he was willing even to become a prisoner for Christ's sake.

The Revelation Given to Paul (3:2-6)

Paul added a phrase to his description of himself in verse 1. He was "a prisoner of Christ Jesus *for the sake of you Gentiles*" (author's italics).

The Gentiles were somehow the cause of his imprisonment. Understanding how the Gentiles were related to Paul's imprisonment will provide further insight into the dynamics of his life.

We are living in a day when knowledge is power. To know something someone else does not know makes one valuable. Paul's power came in part from the special mystery God revealed to him. Paul understood something others did not understand. What was this secret which had been revealed to Paul? God revealed to Paul that Jews and Gentiles could be reconciled to Him in the very same way. Paul described this revelation from God with two different phrases. He called it "the stewardship of God's grace" (v. 2) and "the mystery" (v. 3).

Partial Revelation in the Past (3:5)

This mystery about which Paul wrote had been anticipated in other generations. In His original promise to Father Abraham, God said, "And in you all the families of the earth shall be blessed" (Gen. 12:3). The prophets also alluded to this mystery. The prophet Isaiah recorded these words of God to His Messiah who was to come, "I will also make You a light of the nations so that My salvation may reach to the end of the earth" (Isa. 49:6). Hosea 1:10 contains this promise from God: "And it will come about that, in the place where it is said to them, 'You are not My people,' It will be said to them, 'You are the sons of the living God.' "

The mystery about which Paul spoke was revealed in some degree to those in other generations. Nevertheless, Paul pointed out the incompleteness of this revelation in the phrase, "which in other generations was not made known to the sons of men" (v. 5). Seers in the past had not comprehended the universality of God's offer of salvation. Consequently, in Paul's day, barriers remained between Jews and Gentiles.

Complete Revelation in the Present (3:6)

The full dimensions of this truth were not clearly understood until the Holy Spirit revealed them to God's people. The "holy apostles" were the original twelve disciples. The "prophets in the Spirit" (v. 5) were those who through the Spirit were given the gift of proclamation. What they began to grasp had been made clear to the apostle Paul.

What is this mystery God revealed to Paul? What is this truth which the saints of the old covenant never fully realized but now had been revealed to the apostles and prophets of the new covenant? Paul finally described this truth in verse 6. God revealed to Paul that the Gentiles were "fellow heirs," "fellow members," and "fellow partakers."

That statement does not have the same impact on us today as it had on the first Christians. To these Jewish Christians this was a revolutionary idea. The impact of it is most clearly expressed by William Hendriksen, "Paul makes it very clear that God's unveiled secret ('mystery') has to do not merely with an alliance of Jew and Gentile, or perhaps a friendly agreement to live together in peace, or even an outward combination or partnership, but, on the contrary, with a complete and permanent fusion, a perfect spiritual union of formerly clashing elements into one new organism, even a new humanity."[4] In this new spiritual union, the privileges initially reserved for the Jews were now open to the Gentiles.

Fellow heirs.—An heir is one who has an inheritance coming. As children of God, the Jews were heirs to all the promises of God. Now, Paul said, the Gentiles share that inheritance. Being a Jew or a Gentile was neither an asset nor a liability in the church. Jews and Gentiles alike who were in Christ shared God's riches.

Fellow members of the body.—The Gentile had the same standing before God and the same opportunities for service as did the Jew. Our physical birth determines whether we are black or white, American or Russian. Our spiritual birth determines our relationship with God. All who are in Christ are a part of the family of God.

Fellow partakers of the promise.—The promise to which Paul referred is the promise of salvation. Gentiles can experience salvation to the same degree and in the same way as can the Jews. The Gentiles did not have to become Jews before they could become Christians. They could become Christians in the same way Jews could—through personal faith in and commitment to Jesus Christ.

We need to be captured again by the universal availability of the gospel. This is the open invitation of the New Testament. Not the suggestion that all *will* be saved but the good news that all *can* be saved. No one is excluded from the invitation of the gospel. Whosoever will may come!

The Reconciliation Implemented in Paul (3:7)

Mention of the word "gospel" reminded Paul he had been called to share that gospel with the Gentiles so they could be reconciled to God. So Paul mentioned in verse 7 the reconciliation which was implemented in him. Notice three thoughts in this verse.

God Enlisted Paul for this Special Assignment (3:7)

God called Paul to preach the gospel to the Gentiles. Paul did not volunteer for the assignment. He did not strive for the assignment. God gave it to him. Paul said, "I was made a minister" (v. 7). Throughout the ages, God has called individual Christians to specific assignments in His kingdom work, just like He did Paul.

A number of years ago a study was done on individuals who were involved in religious work on a full-time basis. The study focused on their motives for being involved in a religious profession. According to the study, a majority of people who serve in full-time religious jobs were there because of guilt.[5] Perhaps that is why so many in the ministry today are burning out, because they were not enlisted for this special assignment by God but by their guilt. The only permanent motivation for ministry is the belief God called us to that assignment.

God Equipped Paul for This Special Assignment (3:7)

When God called Paul to a specific ministry, He gave him the gifts he needed to carry out that ministry. Paul carried out his assignment "according to the gift of God's grace" (v. 7). Whom God calls, God equips. That is simple but significant truth we need to remember. If God opens a door of opportunity for us, if He leads us to do something, He will provide what we need to fulfill that responsibility. God still gives gifts to individual Christians today, just like He did Paul.

A young lady asked Arthur Rubinstein, the piano virtuoso, to listen to her playing. He consented. When she finished, she asked, "What do you think I should do now?" Rubinstein responded, "Get married!" Nothing creates more misery than for a person to attempt something for which he has no gifts. This is not necessary in Christian ministry, for the Lord gifts each of us adequately to fulfill the assignment to which He has called us.

God Empowered Paul for This Special Assignment (3:7)

Paul carried out this special assignment "according to the working of His power" (v. 7). When God called Paul to a specific ministry, He provided the power he needed to carry out that ministry. We not only need to know how to do something. We also need the power to do it. God provides that power. We do not have to carry out our responsibilities as Christians in our own weak way. We can do them in God's powerful way. God still empowers Christians today, just like He did Paul.

A story from India tells of a mouse who was terrified of cats until a magician agreed to transform him into a cat. That solved the problem until the new cat met a dog, so the magician turned him into a dog. That worked until the new dog met a tiger, so the magician turned him into a tiger. That helped until the tiger met a hunter. The mouse-turned-cat-turned-dog-turned tiger complained to the magician again. This time, the magician turned him back into a mouse saying, "You have the body of a tiger, but you still have the heart of a mouse."[6]

God reverses that process. As Christians, we still have the body of a human being, but we have been given the heart of the Spirit. The Spirit empowers us to use the gifts God has given to carry out the assignment to which we have been called.

The Response Given by Paul (3:8-10)

God gave Paul a special revelation and then a special assignment. However, this did not make Paul proud. Instead, it humbled him. Paul did not consider himself the greatest saint because of this revelation. Instead, he described himself as "the very least of all saints."

This was not a once-in-a-lifetime sentiment but an opinion Paul repeatedly expressed. In Roman 7:18, Paul said, "For I know that nothing good dwells in me, that is, in my flesh." In 1 Corinthians 15:10, Paul wrote, "But by the grace of God I am what I am." To the Philippian Christians, Paul said at the end of his fruitful ministry, "Brethren, I do not regard myself as having laid hold of it yet" (3:13). To young Timothy, Paul wrote, "It is a trustworthy statement, deserving full acceptance, that Christ Jesus came into the world to save sinners, among whom I am foremost of all" (1 Tim. 1:15).

Paul, who in the opinion of Christian historians was the greatest of the saints, was in his own estimation the least of the saints. Paul expressed in his life true humility, not the kind of false humility we find in those who say they are nothing but who really believe they are something. Paul expressed true humility. Such humility is characterized by three things.

The Right Attitude

A humble person has the right attitude. He knows the Source of his gifts.

Francis of Assisi (1182-1226) was one of history's greatest saints. When asked why he was so influential and why he had so much power with people, he replied, "I've been thinking about that myself lately, and this is why. The Lord looked down from heaven and said, 'Where can I find the weakest, the littlest, the meanest man on the face of the earth?' Then he saw me and said, 'I've found him, and now I'll work through him. He won't be proud of it. He'll see that I am using him because of his littleness and insignificance.' "[7]

That is humility. Not a person who says, "I can do nothing," but one who says, "I can do all things but it is only because of Christ working in me." That spirit of true humility led Paul to say in 2 Corinthians 4:7,

"But we have this treasure in earthen vessels that the surpassing greatness of the power may be of God and not from ourselves."

The Right Focus

A humble person has the right focus—not on himself but on Christ.

Arguments have ensued through the centuries about which is greater: feminine vanity or masculine ego. At a dinner party a man suggested women were much more vain than men. The agreeable hostess said, "I thoroughly agree with you. For instance, one of the most handsome men in this room right now has not noticed his necktie is crooked." Immediately, ten men nervously checked to see if their ties were straight!

The humble person does not think lowly of himself. He simply does not think of himself at all. The opposite of humility is pride. The antidote for pride is to move our eyes off ourselves and focus them on Christ.

The Right Perspective

A humble person has the right perspective. He accepts his limitations in light of the greatness of God. Charlie Shedd told about his last year in seminary when he felt he had arrived. He thought more highly of himself than he should. His professor sensed the growing pride in Charlie so he called him to the front of the room one day. To his side he called the shortest man in the student body. The professor said, "Shedd, physically you are the biggest man around. Kennedy here is small. In fact, he is the smallest man in the school. When you go to Colorado to preach this summer, I hope you have a good time. But one day, for your own good, stand together at the foot of Pike's Peak and notice that compared to the mountain, neither of you is very big."[8]

That is humility. Not a person who thinks others are more important than him but one who recognizes we all pale into insignificance in the presence of the One who holds the whole world in His hands.

Winston Churchill (1874-1965) had little admiration for his political rival, Clement Attlee, and rarely had anything good to say about him. His friends were surprised, therefore, when he reputedly volunteered the information, "Clement Attlee is a very humble man." After a suitable pause, Churchill added with a twinkle in his eye, "Of course, he has a lot to be humble about!" So do we all.

The Result Achieved Through Paul (3:11-13)

When Paul carried out the assignment given to him and proclaimed the truth revealed to him, certain things resulted. Paul summarized these benefits for all Christians as we carry out our God-given assignments.

Boldness (3:12)

We have been given boldness *(parresian)*. This word comes from two Greek words which mean all and telling. A bold person, therefore, is one who tells all. He is completely frank in expressing his opinion. Through Christ we can come boldly into God's presence and tell Him everything. And we can boldly declare the truth about Him to everyone.

Some Christians hesitate to be bold because they believe such boldness to be in conflict with the spirit of humility we Christians are supposed to display. Humility and boldness are not opposites. Boldness grows out of humility. When through submission to Christ, we come into the presence of God and have fellowship with Him, when we realize we are what we are because of the grace of God, when we realize the source of our gifts is not us but God, that does not make us timid. It makes us bold.

When our youth group returns from their mission trip each year, they report to the church. When they do, they exhibit great boldness as they stand before the congregation and share what Christ means to their lives. Some of our young people give a clear, compelling witness for Christ at these report services for the first time. The reason for their boldness is the renewed access to God through Jesus Christ they have experienced on the mission trip. Time spent with God produces a boldness within.

Access (3:12)

We also have been given access *(prosagogen)*. This word described the process of bringing a man into the presence of a king or introducing a speaker to an assembly. It not only means to come into someone's presence but to have that someone give you his attention. Through Christ, we can come into God's very presence and He gives you His attention.

Have you ever tried to contact a prominent person whom you did not know? Several years ago in Pensacola we were making plans for our annual Challenger Award Banquet which recognized the high-school football teams in our area. Each year, we invited college football players who were also Christians to come share their testimony at the banquet. We wanted several of the University of Alabama players to come. For them to come, we had to obtain Coach Paul "Bear" Bryant's permission. I tried every way I knew to contact him by phone but was never able to make connection. One day, Jet Rogers came by my office. Jet was a local coach who had formerly coached with "Bear" Bryant. I told him what I wanted. He picked up the phone and dialed a number. In a few seconds, I was talking on the phone with the legendary coach.

What Jet did for me is an illustration of what Christ does for us in our relationship with God. Jesus is called "the door" in John 10:7, the "mediator" in 1 Timothy 2:5, the "high priest" in Hebrews 4:14, "the way" in John 14:6. Each of these designations declares the same truth Paul declared in our text. Jesus gives us access to God. He puts us in touch with our Creator.

When Paul carried out his mission and declared the good news of God in Jesus Christ, individuals who responded in faith accessed God.

Community (3:13)

To the Ephesians, Paul described his tribulations as being "on your behalf." He added "they are your glory." What did that mean? Paul was describing the community of faith which makes our lives interrelated. Different denominations are a part of the fabric of church life today. They are different expressions of our unique approaches. But superseding all denominational lines is the community which we share together in Christ.

In France, during World War II, some men took the body of a buddy to a local cemetery. The priest would not let them bury their friend there because he was not a Catholic. The men buried their friend just outside the cemetery fence. The next day they could not find the grave. The priest explained, "The first part of the night I stayed awake, sorry for what I had told you. The second part of the night I spent moving the fence." That is what Jesus did. He moved the fence of God's love so it would include every person.

For Discussion

1. What are some ways in which we sacrifice for the cause of Christ today?

2. Are all Christians equal before God? If so, why? If not, why not?

3. To what ministry has God called you? Does God call every Christian to a specific ministry?

4. How does humility manifest itself in a Christian today? Do you know someone who displays this kind of humility?

5. Why are we as Christians not more bold in the expression of our Christian faith?

6 | Equal to the Opportunity

Ephesians 3:14-21

I remember an old story of a boy who fell into a barrel of molasses. As he was going under, he prayed, "Lord, make my tongue equal to the opportunity!" That is what Paul wanted for his Christian friends in Ephesus. He wanted them to be equal to the opportunity God placed before them. That was the essence of his prayer for them in our text.

Remember the context. Paul concluded the second chapter with a glorious description of the church. When the full impact of that picture gripped Paul's mind—the unparalleled potential within the Ephesian Christians and the unquestionable challenge before them—Paul burst into a prayer. However, as he started to pray, he was sidetracked on a thought. In this interlude, covering verses 2-13, Paul revealed some interesting insights into his life. After the interlude, Paul returned to his main thought in verse 14. Verse 14, then, is a continuation of verse 1. Because of what God gave the church to do, Paul prayed the Ephesians would be equal to the opportunity before them. What would it take?

Courage (3:16)

What had to happen before these Ephesians were equal to the opportunity before them? They had to be strengthened. They had to have power. So Paul prayed they would "be strengthened with power through His Spirit in the inner man."

Courage is a scarce commodity in today's world. Fear is more often the determining force in our lives. For example, two men were hunting a lion. They came to the tracks of what appeared to be the largest lion in the jungle. One hunter said to the other, "You go that way to see where he went. I'll go this way to see where he came from!" That is our usual approach, to run away from the challenges of our life. However, to be equal to the opportunity before us we must not be cowardly but courageous, not timid but bold, not weak but strong. We must be "strengthened with power." How can that happen? And where does it happen?

52

How?

How can we be courageous when confronted by both opportunity and opposition? This courage comes "through His Spirit" (v. 16). We cannot face our opposition, we cannot fulfill our opportunity, without God's help. We cannot do it on our own. We must have God's strength.

A dozen times each day, in the context of my family when the children were small, I was given analogies of this truth. When three-year-old Marty woke up in the morning he wanted to put his clothes on, but he could not do it on his own. We had to help. Five-year-old Cara could not remove the knot from the laces on her tennis shoe by herself, so we had to help. Eight-year-old Collin wanted to build a fort in the backyard but he could not do it on his own. So we had to help. Ten-year-old Jay came home from school upset because of something said to him. He could not understand it. So we had to explain.

As parents do for their children, our Heavenly Father does for us. He strengthens us by His Spirit. We simply cannot make it without His help. The sooner we realize and admit our dependence upon God and our need for Him, the sooner we will be able to realize the dreams placed before us and fulfill the destiny given to us.

Where?

Where does God strengthen us? This strengthening comes "in the inner man" (v. 16). What does this mean? The inner man includes our reason, conscience, and will. God strengthens our reason so we can be less at the mercy of our passions, instincts, and desires. God strengthens our consciences so we can be more sensitive to His will and thus better able to discern between right and wrong. God strengthens our wills so we can have the inner courage to follow through on the things our reason and our conscience tell us to do.

What will make us equal to the opportunity before us? Not our family name, circumstances, connections to our bank account, physical condition, past experience, or education, only the condition of our inner man. That's why God strengthens the inner man with His Spirit. By a daily dependence on God, we can know the reality Paul described in 2 Corinthians 4:16: "Therefore we do not lost heart, but though our outer man is decaying, yet our inner man is being renewed day by day."

Commitment (3:17)

Notice Paul's wonderful prayer for the Ephesians in verse 17. He prayed that "Christ may dwell in your hearts through faith." *The Ampli-*

fied Bible helps us with the meaning of the word "dwell"—*katoikesai.* *The Amplified Bible* translates the verse: "May Christ through your faith [actually] dwell (settle down, abide, make His permanent home) in your hearts!" Paul prayed that Christ will feel at home as He dwells in our lives.

When we become Christians, God in His Spirit indwells us. Our lives become the permanent dwelling place of our God. Jesus expressed this truth in John 14:23: "If anyone loves Me, he will keep My word; and My Father will love him, and We will come to him, and make Our abode with him." To be adequate for the opportunities God gives to us, we need to allow the One who lives within us to settle down in our life. Is Christ comfortable in our life? Does He feel at home?

The Relationships

Does Christ feel at home with the relationships of our lives? The statement "no man is an island" is more than a cliché. It is a truth about life. No person can live apart from relationships with other people. The establishment of relationships with fellow human beings is a key element in every normal life. We all have a relationship hunger to be filled. However, we can have bad relationships as well as good relationships. Some relationships honor God, and other relationships are displeasing to God. Even in honorable relationships such as with our wives, children, and friends, we can carry these out in honorable or dishonorable ways.

Can Christ comfortably be part of all the relationships of our lives? Can He feel at home with the way we treat other people? The answers will provide an accurate measure of the depth of our commitment.

The Attitudes

Does Christ feel at home with the attitudes of our lives? The Bible challenges us with this appeal: "Have this attitude in yourselves which was also in Christ Jesus" (Phil. 2:5). Do we have His attitude toward the work of God when Jesus said, "My food is to do the will of Him who sent me, and to accomplish His work" (John 4:34)? Do we have His attitude toward others when He said, "The Son of Man did not come to be served, but to serve, and to give His life a ransom for many" (Matt. 20:28)? Do we have His attitude toward our enemies when He said, "Love your enemies and pray for those who persecute you" (5:44)?

The list can go on endlessly. Does Jesus feel comfortable with our finances, with our language, with our leisure time, with the way we do our job, with the way we take care of ourself physically? Paul prayed that Jesus might dwell in our lives, but the only way He can do that is if He feels comfortable with the attitudes we exhibit. Jesus dwells in the life of every believer. That comes as the result of our conversion. The question which reveals the level of our commitment as Christians is simply this: "Does Jesus feel at home in our lives?"

Comprehension (3:18-19a)

When a little boy found a dead squirrel in the street, the boy's father used this event to teach his son about safety. He used the dead squirrel to explain what could happen to him if he ran into the street when cars were coming. A few days later, his mother fastened his seat belt and then reminded him it was for his own safety. A person could be killed in a car wreck. "I know," the little boy replied, "I don't want to do that because when you die, you turn into a squirrel!"

Many adults are equally confused about life and death. In fact, many of the shortcomings in the Christian life come because of our misunderstanding of God. To be equal to the opportunity, the Ephesian Christians needed more than a deep level of courage and a high level of commitment. They also needed to have a full comprehension of God.

Paul used two key words. He wanted the Ephesians to comprehend the love of God (v. 18). This word *(katalabesthai)* means to lay hold of, to seize, to take possession of. It means to understand something with the mind. Paul also wanted the Ephesians to know the love of Christ (v. 19). This word *(ginonaite)* refers to knowledge gained by experience. Thus, Paul wanted the Ephesians to comprehend with their minds and experience in their lives the full dimensions of the love of God. Paul then described the love of God they needed to comprehend.

Inescapable (3:18)

The love of God is an inescapable love. Paul spoke of "the breadth and length and height and depth" of God's love. What do these dimensions mean?

One of the early church fathers described the love of Christ as reaching up to touch the angels, and reaching down to include even the evil spirits in hell. In its length, it covers those who are striving on the upward way. In its breadth, it covers those who are drifting and wandering away from Christ on evil paths.

William Barclay made this suggestion. The length of God's love is its scope from eternity to eternity. The breadth of God's love refers to its inclusion of all people, Jew and Gentile alike. The height of God's love refers to where we are in Christ, risen to sit together with Him in heavenly places. The depth of God's love refers to the living death out of which God has called us.[1]

Probably, all of these explanations go beyond what Paul originally intended. Paul was simply declaring the unlimited reach of God's love. No one is outside the love of God. No place is outside the reach of God's love. Paul wanted the Ephesian Christians to understand that wherever they were, they were right in the middle of God's love, for it is inescapable.

Inexhaustible (3:19)

The love of Christ "surpasses knowledge." This Greek word *(huperballousan)* means to throw over or beyond, to transcend or to exceed. This does not mean the love of God cannot be known at all. It means all of the love of God cannot be known. No matter how much the Christian experiences the love of God, oceans of love in the great heart of God remain that we have not yet experienced. As the songwriter said, "The love of God is greater far than tongue or pen can ever tell." It is inexhaustible.

Bill Blackburn tells of a family with a strained relationship between the mother and the sixteen-year-old daughter, Jennifer. Jennifer had an older sister and a younger brother. The middle-child syndrome affected her and by the time she was in middle school, Jennifer drifted away from the family. Eventually, her hunger for attention drove her to an attempted suicide. On her sixteenth birthday, Jennifer took an overdose of pills. The mother came home and found her. After a quick trip to the hospital to have Jennifer's stomach pumped, Jennifer entered counseling.

However, the delinquent behavior and the threat of suicide continued. One morning Jennifer's mother woke early, especially distraught. She spent some time in prayer and Bible study. She was impressed during that time to reach out once more to Jennifer and assure her of her love. While Jennifer was dressing for school, her mother entered her room and delivered an assurance that somehow turned Jennifer's life around. She told her sixteen-year-old daughter, "Jenny, I don't know why you've been going through all the things you have, but I want you to know that there's nothing you can do to make me stop loving you."[2] That is the assurance Paul delivered to the Ephesians. Nothing they could do would ever make God stop loving them. His love is inexhaustible.

To be equal to the opportunity God places before us we need to comprehend with our minds and experience in our lives the inescapable, inexhaustible dimensions of the love of God.

Completion (3:19b-21)

To be equal to the opportunity, we also need to experience the fullness which comes from Christ. Paul prayed for the Ephesians to "be filled up to all the fulness of God." That might seem like an impossible attainment until we hear what Paul said about the resource which makes it possible.

The Resource (3:20)

God is the One who brings about this completion. In one of the most remarkable statements in the New Testament, Paul expressed God's adequacy. With word stacked upon word Paul painted an incredible picture of God.

Paul began with the simple assertion: God is able. That in itself would be sufficient to give us security. God is able. Yet, Paul went further. God is able to provide everything we ask Him for. That is certainly a sufficient expression of the adequacy of God. Nevertheless, Paul went further still. He said God is not only able to provide that for which we ask, but also He can supply anything we even think about. All of us think about possibilities we are afraid to ask for. What a promise. All the dreams which ever pass through our minds, all the things we have thought of accomplishing for God in our wildest imagination—God is able to do those things. God is able to supply everything we need, to respond to everything we ask, and to provide everything we have ever thought about. What a picture. Yet, there is more.

Paul said God is not only able to do those things, but He is also able to go beyond all of those things. Paul formed a unique compound out of three words: *huper* which means above or beyond; *ek* which intensifies the force of the verb to which it is connected to a level of perfection; and *perissou* which means "to exceed to a degree that you go beyond all things." *Huperekperissou* literally means to go beyond all things in an inexhaustible way.

Our God is able! His power is beyond imagination. His resources exceed our ability even to comprehend. And those resources are available to us. Whatever we need, God is able to provide it. Whatever we are called to do, God is able to help us accomplish it. Whatever task we have before us, God will empower us to complete it. Whatever we dream for our church or for our lives, God is able to help us realize our dreams. God is able.

The Result (3:21)

Why has this incredible resource been made available to us? Paul gave the answer in verse 21: "To Him be the glory in the church and in Christ Jesus to all generations forever and ever." We are given God's power not to magnify self, not to gratify our personal wants, not to dazzle the world, but to bring glory to God. How can we glorify God?

By the way we worship.—The psalmist said, "Whoso offereth praise glorifieth me" (Ps. 50:23, KJV). Not just by being present in worship but by participating enthusiastically in worship, we honor God.

By the way we live.—Jesus gave this challenge in the Sermon on the Mount: "Let your light shine before men in such a way that they may see your good works, and glorify your Father who is in heaven" (Matt. 5:16). We are not saved by our works but we are saved for works. As we live the Christian life, we honor God.

By the way we give.—Paul emphasized this truth in the instructions he wrote to the Corinthians. He told the Corinthians, "Because of the proof given by this ministry they will glorify God for your obedience to your confession of the gospel of Christ, and for the liberality of your contribution to them and to all" (2 Cor. 9:13). As we give liberally to God so His work can prosper, we honor God.

By the way we relate.—A rigid barrier existed in the New Testament world between the Jews and the Gentiles. When the gospel was proclaimed, this barrier began to disintegrate. After Peter preached to the Gentile Cornelius and his entire family was converted, Peter reported to the church in Jerusalem. After he described the conversion of the Gentiles and the breaking down of the barrier between the Jew and the Gentile, the Bible says, "And when they heard this, they quieted down, and glorified God" (Acts 11:18). As we relate to all individuals through the love of Christ, we honor God.

Conclusion

Newscaster Morton Dean was not always successful. In high school, he was a substitute on the football team. He did not play often. During one crucial game, he had to go in with his team a yard and a half from the goal line. Before his coach sent him in, he said, "Throw a jump pass." As he ran out onto the field, he rehearsed in his mind what he needed to do. Take the snap, step back, jump up, and pop the ball to the end. Correct execution would lead to success and new standing for Morton on the team. This was his big moment. Instead of being a dream come true, however, Morton Dean's big moment turned into a nightmare. He fumbled, the team did not score, and the game was lost. Although he relived this horrible experience for years to come, some benefit came from it. He learned a lesson from his father in this experience that helped him throughout his life. His father said, "Morton, you've got to be prepared to come off the bench."[3]

As Christians, we never know when our big moment will come, so we need to be prepared. We need to prepare ourselves spiritually, and then pray, at each moment, we will be equal to the opportunity God gives to us.

For Discussion

1. How can we find courage for facing the challenges of life today?
2. What can we do to make God feel more at home in our lives?
3. How would you describe the love of God? What has been the most unusual experience of God's love in your own life?
4. Why do we not experience more fully the power of God which is available to us as Christians?
5. How can we glorify God in our lives?

7 | Growing Up in Christ

Ephesians 4:1-16

In the first three chapters of the epistle, Paul dealt with the doctrines of the Christian life. In the last three chapters, he dealt with the duties of the Christian life. In the first three chapters, he talked about the riches of the Christian. In the last three chapters, he talked about the responsibilities of the Christian. In the first half, he told what the Christian believes. In the second half, he told how the Christian behaves. To properly understand these two dimensions, they have to be kept in order. The doctrine leads to the duties. The belief results in the behavior. That is why Paul began chapter 4 with the word "therefore." Because we believe certain things, we should behave in certain ways. The ultimate goal of this belief and behavior is for us to grow up into mature Christians. In this section, Paul described the steps involved in growing up in Christ.

Developing the Character of the Christian Life (4:1-3)

Because of what we believe, the first thing we should do is "to walk in a manner worthy of the calling to which we have been called" (v. 1). The word "walk" *(peripatesai)* means more than to walk. It means to conduct oneself or to order one's behavior. The word "worthy" *(axios)* means having the weight of another thing. Picture an old set of scales with a bar across the top, with two containers hanging by a chain from the ends of the bar. In one of the containers is the life God expects a Christian to live. In the other container is our life. The two should be equal. Our life ought to weigh as much as the life God expects us to live.

We are to so conduct our daily behavior that we measure up to God's expectations of us. What are God's expectations? How will we know if we are measuring up? Paul gave some clues in verses 2-3.

Humility (4:2)

God expects humility to be a part of our character. In the ancient world, humility *(tapeinophrosunes)* was not considered a virtue. Greatness was a virtue; humility was a cowering, cringing approach to life

60

which was to be avoided. Yet, Christ demonstrated humility as a quality to be desired, and He challenged His disciples to live in humility.

Humility comes from two sources: a proper understanding of God and a proper understanding of ourselves. A proper understanding of God recognizes Him as being the God who created the world and who is in charge of it, One who is above all other powers and things. A proper understanding of ourselves recognizes the weakness, the inadequacies, the shortcomings of our lives. Humility is the recognition that our worth and value are found not in ourselves—because of our obvious weakness—but in God—because of His obvious strength. Humility is understood when we contrast it with two other attitudes we often have as we face life.

Self-hate.—Amazingly, many people struggle with a low self-esteem. They just do not like themselves. They do not think much of themselves. Therefore, they continually put themselves down. What is even sadder is when Christians do this and think this is the attitude they are supposed to have. The Bible says we are to have humility, but humility is not self-hate.

Self-confidence.—For some, their theme song is, "I don't need anybody. I can take care of my own life. I am the captain of my ship. I am the master of my fate." They face life with the declaration, "I can do all things." That is pride, and pride is to be avoided in the Christian life. We are not to think more highly of ourselves than we should or more lowly of ourselves than we should. We are to have humility. Humility does not say, "I can do nothing," like self-hate does. Neither does it say, "I can do all things," like self-confidence says. Humility says, "I can do all things, but it is only because of the power of God which is at work within me." Humility is part of the expected character of a Christian.

Gentleness (4:2)

Gentleness is also essential to Christian character. What does "gentleness" *(praetetos)* mean? According to Aristotle, this word referred to a person who lived at the midpoint between excessive anger and complete passivity. This person was at times angry, but only at the right time and for the right reason. This person was under control.[1] This Greek word was also used to describe an animal that had been trained until it was completely under discipline. Again, the idea is of control.

Gentleness, then, describes a person who lives under control. His emotions are under control. His thoughts are under control. His tongue is under control. His desires are under control. He is a controlled person.

Patience (4:2)

Christian character also includes patience. The word "patience" *(makrothumias)* is used most often to describe a person's reaction to another person who has mistreated him. It speaks of the spirit of a person who refuses to retaliate. It is the spirit which bears with everything anyone can do to it. The patient person is a person with a long fuse.

The word, which appears frequently in reference to God, is usually translated "longsuffering." The longsuffering of God is what keeps God from wiping out the world because of our sin. He bears with mankind, He endures mankind's rebellion, He refuses to retaliate with anger but instead loves us—all because of His longsuffering. This is to be our attitude toward those who do us evil. We are to bear up under it without retaliating.

Love (4:2)

Paul explained how the Christian could have patience toward others in the fourth characteristic. We are to show "forbearance to one another in love." The Christian is to walk in humility, in gentleness, in patience, and fourth in "love" *(agape)*.

The Greek words for "love" are sometimes used interchangeably in the New Testament, so it is unsafe to take too strong a position on the unique meaning of each word. Nevertheless, in its most common usage, *agape* speaks of a kind of love which seeks the highest good of another person, regardless of what that person does. With that kind of love we are to love other Christians.

Notice, this love is not based on feeling but on commitment. This kind of love does not grow out of our feelings. It grows out of our commitment to love other people in the same way Jesus loves us. That commitment is the foundation for Christian love.

Peace (4:3)

Peace is also a part of Christian character. We live in peace only when we move self from the center of things. When a husband and wife are at war with each other, it is because one of them or both of them has put self in the center. When a church experiences a division, it is because one of the members or a group of the members have put self in the center. When self is at the center, our desires, feelings, and prestige are more important than anything else. On the other hand, when we put Christ at the center, His desires are more important than ours. The feelings of others are as important as ours. Glorifying God is more important than glorifying ourselves. When Christ is in the center, we will be able to walk together in peace.

When we walk in peace and humility, relating to others with gentleness and patience and love, we will be displaying the proper Christian character.

Discovering the Commonalities of the Christian Life (4:4-6)

Ecumenism has been a hot topic for several decades. The word refers to the attempts to cross denominational lines in an effort to unite all Christians in a common body. Although ecumenism is on the wane, the underlying theme of unity among Christians must not be lost. Granted, denominations have different characteristics, and granted, different opinions on specific doctrines prevail among Christians. Nevertheless, all Christians are bound together by certain elements they share. Paul outlined these commonalities of the Christian life in this section.

One Body (4:4)

What did Paul mean when he said we are one body? He was referring to a reality that supersedes the local body of believers to which we belong and the denominational affiliation we claim. This reality is the universal body of believers under the headship of Christ. This does not mean the local body of believers is not important, nor does it mean a Christian is justified in not joining with some local congregation of believers.

A spiritually minded man told the preacher he wanted to sing in the church's choir although he did not want to join the church. He quickly added he was a member of the great invisible church. The pastor responded, "If you are a member of the great invisible church why don't you just sing in the great invisible choir?"

Every Christian should belong to a local congregation of believers. Yet, we must never forget this is not all there is. Every Christian is a member of a larger body, the body of Christ, which is composed of every Christian in every church who lives under the Lordship of Christ.

One Spirit (4:4)

Paul also said we have one spirit. Many conflicting ideas are going around today about the Holy Spirit. What we have in common, however, the point at which we find our unity, is our common testimony that what we do is the result of the work of God's Spirit within us. Our service, our work, and our accomplishments are not of mankind but God. As breath is to the body, so is the Spirit to the body of Christ. He gives us our vitality, life, and power.

One Hope (4:4)

What was Paul referring to when he stated we have one hope? Some believe he was referring to the second coming of Christ. All Christians have the hope of the return of the Lord. Another interesting suggestion has been made. Perhaps Paul was referring to our purpose with the phrase "hope of our calling." All Christians, regardless of our denominational affiliation, have one purpose, one goal in mind: to have a world redeemed by Christ. The hope of our calling is to see the day when "every knee should bow . . . and every tongue should confess that Jesus Christ is Lord" (Phil. 2:10-11).

One Lord (4:5)

The earliest creed of the church was simply, "Jesus is Lord." The young man who wanted to show his religious faith by purchasing stained-glass contact lens had the right intention but the wrong idea! We do need to publicly demonstrate our faith, and the way we do it is through our acceptance of Jesus as Lord.

One Faith (4:5)

Paul was not referring here to the contents of faith as if to say every Christian believes the identical things about every element of our faith. The word "faith" can refer to an object or to an attitude. Paul probably had the latter in mind. What brings all Christians together in unity is not our creed but our commitment. The act of surrender to Christ is one thing common to all Christians.

One Baptism (4:5)

We need to make a distinction between the form of baptism and its meaning. Concerning the form of baptism, Christians have different opinions. A Baptist and Methodist were arguing about the form of baptism. The Baptist declared, "It's all the way under, or it is no good!"

The Methodist asked, "What about up to the waist?"

"No," the Baptist responded. "It has to be all the way under."

"What about everything except the top of the head?"

"No," the Baptist replied, "that won't do either. It has to be all the way under."

"Well," the Methodist countered, "You just proved my point. It's the water on the top of the head that really counts!"

Paul was not talking about the form of baptism but its meaning. Baptism is a public, outward expression of an inward commitment to Christ. In Paul's day, a soldier could join the Roman army only if he took an oath that he would be true forever to his emperor and king. Likewise, a person can enter the Christian church in only one way—through a public confession of Christ which is symbolized in baptism. Secret discipleship is impossible, for either the secrecy will destroy the discipleship or the discipleship will destroy the secrecy.

One God (4:6)

What ties us together as Christians, most of all, is the fact that we all have one God. Through our public faith in the Lord Christ we become a part of the family of God. During the Second World War, a Catholic chaplain came beside a dying soldier who was a Presbyterian. The boy said, "But I don't belong to your church." "That's all right," the priest replied, "you belong to my God." And so do all Christians. Although each denomination has its distinctiveness and every church has its uniqueness, Christians have more commonalities than contrasts. Paul urged the Ephesians to come together around these commonalities.

Demonstrating the Calling of the Christian Life (4:7-13)

The foundational statement and summary of this section are found in verse 7. Paul said, "But to each one of us grace was given according to the measure of Christ's gift." Remember the discussion which preceded this verse. In verses 4-6, Paul declared the unity of the church. There is one body, one Spirit, one hope, one Lord, one faith, one baptism, and one God over all. All of us are a part of one body. However, just as a body has different parts, even so the body of Christ has different parts. The unity of the church does not rule out diversity within the body. All of us are a part of the body of Christ, but each of us, individually, is given a gift from Christ. Paul's statement in verse 7 implies several truths we need to nail down.

Each of Us Has a Spiritual Gift (4:7)

Spiritual gifts are not given to some but withheld from others. Paul said, "To each one of us" these spiritual gifts are given. Have you ever wondered what your spiritual gift is? Do you have the gift of preaching? Of administration? Of helps? Of giving? Of encouragement? What is your spiritual gift? That is an important question, for Paul declared each of us has one.

Spiritual Gifts Come as a Result of God's Grace (4:7)

Paul said, "To each one of us grace was given." What does the word "grace" mean? It refers to something which is given to us that we neither earn nor deserve. Our spiritual gifts are not the product of our own skill or ingenuity. Our spiritual gifts are the product of God's grace. They are not abilities we develop. They are gifts we receive.

All the Gifts Are Important (4:7)

Paul said these gifts were "given according to the measure of Christ's gift." That is, they are measured gifts. No one gift is more important than any other gift. A Christian who has a particular gift is not more important than another Christian with a different gift. They are all important, for each is measured out by Jesus Christ Himself.

Christ Makes Possible These Spiritual Gifts (4:8-10)

The reason Jesus is able to give us spiritual gifts is because He faced the enemies of mankind, defeated them, and now shares the spoils of victory with those who believe in Him.

This mention of Jesus ascending on high led Paul to make a side remark that Jesus "descended into the lower parts of the earth" (v. 9). What does this mean? Perhaps it was a reference to Jesus' burial. The descent of Jesus was His descent into the tomb provided by Joseph in the garden. Or, maybe it was a reference to Jesus' descent into hell, between the time of His death and resurrection. During this descent into hell, Jesus taunted the devil with His victory, preached to some of the lost, and released the Old Testament saints from hades. It could have been a reference to Jesus' incarnation into the world, simply stating that Jesus came to earth. Another possibility is that this was a reference to the humiliation of Jesus' incarnation. The only reason Jesus was able to ascend to the Father with such glory and be welcomed as victor over sin and death is that Jesus had borne the sins of mankind in His humiliating death on the cross.[2]

Of the four suggestions, the fourth seems to be the clearest and best. It was not the burial of Jesus but His death that was the key event to which New Testament writers refer. There is no clear reference in the New Testament that Jesus actually descended to hell during the interval between His death and resurrection. And if Paul was referring to Jesus' incarnation, there are many clearer ways he could have expressed it. Paul seemed to be saying the same thing here as he said in Philippians 2:8: "And being found in appearance as a man, He humbled Himself by becoming obedient to the point of death, even death on a cross. Therefore also God highly exalted Him." In the Philippian passage, we have the descent followed by the ascent, just as we do here in Ephesians.

Because Jesus went through the humiliation of death on the cross for the sins of man and by that death won victory over sin and death, He therefore has the right and the power to bestow spiritual gifts on those who believe in Him.

These Gifts Equip Us for Special Service (4:11)

Paul described in verse 11 different offices or positions in the church. The offices in the church today are not the same as the ones he listed. Nevertheless, the truth remains. These gifts are to be used to carry out responsibilities within the church.

Apostles.—Jesus "gave some as apostles." The word "apostle" *(apostolous)* was used primarily of the original twelve disciples, plus Paul. They were the charter witnesses of the resurrection. Apostles had to have seen Jesus and had to have been witnesses of the resurrection. After these twelve died, there were no other apostles in the strict sense of that word. But Jesus gave to some the gift to be apostles. That they had the opportunity to be apostles was a result of the grace of God.

Prophets.—Jesus "gave some as prophets." The word *prophetas* was used to refer to the occasional organs of inspiration in the early church. A good example is Acts 11:27-28. The Bible says, "Now at this time some prophets came down from Jerusalem to Antioch. And one of them named Agabus stood up and began to indicate by the Spirit that there would certainly be a great famine all over the world."

Prophets traveled from place to place, speaking God's word. Partly because of abuses of the office, and partly because of the development of the canon of Scripture, the office of prophet also faded away. However, in the early church, Jesus gave some the gifts to be prophets.

Evangelists.—Jesus "gave some as evangelists." An evangelist was a traveling missionary, an itinerant preacher. He went from place to place, sharing the gospel and leading people to a commitment to Christ. All of us are to share our witness. And all of us are to do the work of evangelism. However, Jesus gifted some especially to be able to perform this ministry.

Pastors.—Jesus gifted "some as pastors and teachers." The two words refer to one and the same person. This is a reference to ministers of local congregations whose responsibility was to exhort and to teach. Jesus gave to certain ones the gift to pastor local congregations.

These Gifts Bring Blessings to the Church (4:12-13)

Proper use of these gifts will lead to several benefits in the church.

Strength.—We are to use these gifts "for the equipping of the saints for the work of service, to the building up of the body of Christ" (v. 12). The

King James Version renders this verse in three phrases with a comma between each: "For the perfecting of the saints, for the work of the ministry, for the edifying of the body of Christ." Most scholars believe only one comma should be in the verse, after the word "ministry" or "service." The comma distinguishes between the primary purpose of the equipping of the saints and the ultimate purpose.

The saints are equipped to carry out the service of the church. The reason God has given us these spiritual gifts is to be able to serve one another. That is the primary use of our gifts, to carry out deeds of service to one another. But the ultimate purpose is stated in the final phrase in verse 12: "to the building up of the body of Christ." When we use our gifts to perform deeds of service for each other the ultimate result is that the body of Christ will be built up.

Unity.—When every Christian is focused on his gift and what God wants him to do with it, he doesn't have time to complain about others and criticize them. The result is unity. Disunity in the church comes when Christians quit working for Christ and begin to worry about others.

Growth.—When a Christian uses his gift for service to others, it will cause him to grow in his faith. Just like exercising our physical muscles leads to increased physical strength, exercising our spiritual gifts leads to increased spiritual strength. Growth in individual Christians will lead to growth in the body of Christ.

Displaying the Culmination of the Christian Life (4:14-16)

The culmination of the Christian life is maturity. When the church functions as Paul suggested in the preceding verses, every person using his gift for ministering to others and building up the church, maturity will result. When that happens, Paul said, "we are no longer to be children, tossed here and there by waves, and carried about" (v. 14).

Paul mixed his metaphors, taking one from family life and one from the sea. Thinking of the family, Paul said, "we are no longer to be children." The reference to children is the reference to their instability. Their attention span is very short. They do not stay with something for very long. Consequently, they are constantly moving from one thing to another. The other metaphor is from the sea. Perhaps, Paul was thinking of his treacherous journey which brought him to Rome where he was now a prisoner, a journey described in Acts 27. On that journey, the ship on which Paul traveled was often tossed to and fro in the water. In both cases, the image refers to someone or something which is unstable, which constantly goes off on one tangent or another. That kind of instability is a mark of spiritual immaturity. Paul contrasted the immature Christian with the mature Christian.

The Immature Person (4:14)

Paul mentioned two things to which the immature person is particularly susceptible.

Clever ideas.—The immature person is "carried about by every wind of doctrine." Every novel idea that comes along catches the attention of the immature person. He is always taking out after a new truth, a new idea, a new theme. Every time he reads a book, he starts on a new tangent. Every time he attends a Christian conference, he comes back with a new direction for his life.

This is why many immature Christians are being attracted by the New Age movement. The New Age movement is difficult to define, but we see elements of it all around. God and mankind are merged into one entity. In fact, the New Age teaches that man is "god." Many Christians are being caught up by this New Age movement because they are easily attracted by the new and the clever.

Clever people.—The immature person is carried about "by the trickery of men." The word "trickery" *(kubeia)* refers to a cube or a die. Paul had in mind dice-playing where someone would manipulate the dice with tricks in order to win. He added a second phrase: "by craftiness in deceitful scheming." Immature Christians are especially susceptible to trickery. We might say they are gullible. They are not able to look beneath the surface and discern things as they are. Therefore, they are easily sucked in by manipulative people. That partially explains the success of some televangelists who duped thousands of people into sending their money to them. These manipulative and articulate ministers tricked these immature Christians with the use of emotionalism and guilt.

When a person goes back and forth from one new idea to another, when a person goes back and forth from one clever teacher to another, he is an immature Christian. Paul had them in the Ephesian church, and we have them today.

The Mature Person (4:15-16)

In contrast, Paul described a mature person. Several characteristics appear in a mature person.

Keeps a balance between truth and love (v. 15).—The *New American Standard* translation renders the verse to say, "speaking the truth in love." The original text, however, does not say "speaking the truth in love." It simply uses the word *aletheuontes.* Probably the best translation is not "speaking the truth" but "practicing the truth" or "adhering to the truth." We are to adhere to the truth "in love."

Two great enemies threaten a successful Christian life: the lack of integrity and the lack of love. Whenever we depart from the truth and compromise with untruth, we are destroying the foundation of our Christian life. Whenever we quit caring about people and sympathizing with their hurts and needs, we are destroying the force of our Christian life. Many Christians fail to grow because they depart from the truth. Other Christians fail to grow because they do not care about people. When both of those qualities come together in the Christian life, when we adhere to the truth with love and compassion for others, then we will begin to grow in our faith.

Lives under the lordship of Christ (v. 15).—Christian growth has a target. Paul said "we are to grow up in all aspects into Him, who is the head, even Christ." Spiritual growth will begin in our lives when we acknowledge Jesus is in charge of our lives. Jesus is the One who calls the shots. He is the One who sets the guidelines. He is the One who provides the direction. He is the One who supplies the power. Jesus is to be in charge of our lives.

How difficult it is for us to move off the throne of our lives and let Christ take His rightful place there. We want to be Christians, but we want to call the shots. We want to be Christians, but we still want to do everything we desire. We can choose to live like that as Christians, and many do, but the result is stunted spiritual growth. On the other hand, when we allow Christ to be the Lord of our lives and live under His direction, then we will begin to grow in our faith.

Cooperates with others in the church (v. 16).—Growth comes in the context of relationships. Paul said, "from whom the whole body being fitted and held together by that which every joint supplies, according to the proper working of each individual part, causes the growth of the body for the building up of itself in love." The comparison of the church to a body is a common New Testament imagery. The parallels are striking. Just as the human body experiences normal growth when properly supported and held together, so does the church in general, and the individual member of the church in particular.

Christ is the organic head of the church which means He is the one from whom the energy comes for growth. But notice the phrase, "according to the proper working of each individual part." Each individual part of the body, when functioning correctly, generates energy which also helps to build the church up. As we carry out our function as a part of the body of Christ, the body of Christ grows. As a result of the growth of the body, individual Christians grow as well.

For Discussion

1. What does it mean to walk with humility?
2. What commonalities bind all Christians together?
3. What is your spiritual gift? In what way are you using it to further God's kingdom?
4. Why are so many Christians immature in their faith?
5. What are some marks of Christian maturity?

8 | Discarding the Old Self

Ephesians 4:17-22

Categorizing is a favorite pastime of people today. We have categories for everything. For example, modern painters can be divided into five categories: those who paint what they see; those who think they paint what they see; those who paint what they think they see; those who think they paint what they think they see; and those who think they paint! Another example is to divide people on the basis of their thinking: those who think; those who think they think; and those who would rather die than think.

Paul suggested in our text a simple way to classify all people: those who are Christians and those who are not. Those are the only categories. People in these different categories are distinctly different. How is this difference to be reflected?

Some feel the difference should be reflected in our relationships with life in general. This idea spawned the monastic movement of the Middle Ages. Life is evil and the world is bad, according to this viewpoint. Consequently, a Christian distinguishes himself from others by withdrawing from the world. That was the driving force of the medieval monastic movement. In fact, the more pain associated with life on this earth, the more pious this made a person. One monk, Besarion, would not give in to his body's desire for restful sleep and for forty years he would not lie down while sleeping. Simeon Stylites spent thirty years on the top of a sixty-foot pillar and for his deep commitment was exalted to sainthood in the church. In each case, one's dedication was reflected in a total separation from any pleasure of life. Paul did not support such a view. In fact, he warned against such ideas in his Letter to the Colossians (Col. 2:20-22).

Some feel the difference should be reflected in our language. Christians are to talk differently according to this viewpoint. Like the little boy who lived on a farm. The pastor came to visit his parents one day. The pastor sat in the living room in a chair which could not be seen by a little boy dashing into the room. This little boy came into the room holding a rat by

72

the tail. He said to his daddy, "I found this rat by the barn, so I hit it with a two by four. I picked it up and smashed it against the barn. Then I kicked it as hard as I could." About this time, the little boy noticed the preacher sitting in the corner. So he turned to the preacher, and in his most pious tone concluded his monologue by saying, "And then, Preacher, the Lord called him home!" Such pious tones and language are not to be the distinguishing mark of the Christian.

Some feel the difference should be reflected by our outward appearance. Some religious groups in America still wear unique clothes. Other groups do not wear makeup. Still others wear their hair in a certain style. Jesus' statement that what is on the outside is not what counts but what is in the heart discredits any such attempt to distinguish the Christian life by outward appearance.

Christians are to be different, but how? What is to distinguish the Christian from those who do not know Christ? Paul focused on that question in this passage. The pivotal verses in chapter 4 are verses 22 and 24. We are to "lay aside the old self" (v. 22). Then, we are to "put on the new self" (4:24). In other words, a transaction should take place after we become a Christian that is twofold in nature. Certain things need to be put out of our lives. That is the "old self" Paul referred to in verse 22. We will deal with that in this chapter. Then, we need to put on the "new self" which Paul alluded to in verse 24. We'll cover that in chapter 9.

The Christian life does include some negatives. A Christian should put some things out of his life. Paul focused on three of these negatives: wrong thinking, wrong feeling, and wrong acting.

Wrong Thinking (4:17-18)

The first thing we are to put off is wrong thinking. Christians are to think differently from those who do not know Christ. Paul described this unwanted kind of thinking with a number of graphic words.

Those without Christ live "in the futility of their mind" (v. 17). The word "futility" *(mataioteti)* is translated "vanity" in the *King James Version* which presents the idea of excessive pride. The word actually means empty thinking or aimless thinking. Because the old self fills the mind with worthless thoughts, desires, and ambitions which will lead nowhere, those without Christ are confused in their thinking.

Those without Christ are "darkened in their understanding" (v. 18). The word "understanding" *(dianoia)* includes spiritual discernment as well as rational discernment. Because the old self causes a person to live in confusion, affecting both the spiritual discernment and the rational discernment, those without Christ are clouded in their understanding.

Those without Christ are shaped by "the ignorance that is in them" (v. 18). The word "ignorance" *(agnoian)* is the derivative of our word *agnostic*. It means the inability to know. Because the old self clouds the mind and prevents the perception of the truth, those without Christ live in a world excluded from the truth. This clouded thinking of the old self leads to confusion at several points.

Focus on Self Instead of Others

The thinking of the world is decidedly self-centered. And it will continue to be so, according to researcher George Barna. Americans of the nineties will continue to be driven by an ambition to fulfill all our desires. Barna predicts a change from what he calls "conspicuous consumption" to "critical consumption." That is, we will not be as concerned with possessing more as we will be with possessing the best. The emphasis will be on quality instead of quantity. Nevertheless, America will continue to be a narcissistic society where people think first and foremost about self.[1]

We see this self-centeredness displayed in King Saul of Israel. The affection of the people was not directed to him but to a young shepherd boy named David, which sent Saul into a rage of envy. Because Saul could not remove the focus from self, he eventually lost his kingdom.

We see this self-centeredness displayed in the disciples of Jesus. In Mark 9, Jesus shared with the disciples about His impending death. He told them He would be betrayed and would consequently be put to death. How did the disciples respond? What were they concerned about? They were concerned about which one of them was to be the greatest. Because they could not remove the focus from self, they were not prepared when Jesus' death occurred.

We see this self-centeredness displayed in Simon Magus. He was a magician in Samaria who had power and popularity. However, when he observed the power of Peter and John, he desired it for himself. So he approached the disciples with an offer of money for this power they possessed (Acts 8:18-19). Because he could not remove the focus from self, he tried to prostitute the very power of God which had touched his life.

The world puts top priority on looking out for number 1. Jesus countered the self-centeredness of the world with His inescapable challenge: "For whoever wishes to save his life shall lose it; but whoever loses his life for My sake and the gospel's shall save it" (Mark 8:35). We are to put off the wrong thinking which focuses on self.

Focus on the Material Instead of the Spiritual

The thinking of the world is also materialistic. And it is worse today than it has ever been, according to Tony Campolo. He told of an encounter with a delegation from the former Soviet Union who visited the United States. Included in the group were the rectors of two Russian universities as well as the Russian Deputy Minister of Education. Because Campolo was involved in a number of social ministries, he was asked to show the Russian delegation around. In each setting, the Russian visitors interviewed people of all ages, those who were involved in the helping ministries as well as those who were being helped. At the end of the day, Campolo spent some time with the delegation to gain their impressions. The response of the Russian delegation can be summarized in one statement: "These teenagers are so materialistic!"[2]

The world measures everything on the basis of the bottom line. Greed is its driving motive. We see this greed in the desire to have more money. We see this greed in a desire to own more things. The salesman was speaking to this desire when he said to the young housewife, "Let me show you a little item your neighbors said you couldn't afford." We see this greed in the desire to have more control. An old wag suggests, "A rich man's jokes are always funny." Money is power, and the desire to control other people often drives us to earn more, own more, and desire more.

The world focuses on the material. Jesus countered this materialism with His timeless reminder: "For what does it profit a man to gain the whole world, and forfeit his soul?" (Mark 8:36). We are to put off the wrong thinking which focuses on the material.

Focus on the Temporary Instead of the Eternal

Billy could not believe the statement made by his friend Tom. "Tom," he replied in astonishment, "what do you mean when you say our friendship is not strong enough to guarantee this loan? We grew up together. I protected you from the bully who wanted to beat you up. I helped you get through geometry. I talked my sister into marrying you. What do you mean our friendship is not strong enough to guarantee this loan?" Tom replied, "I know about all those things, but the question that concerns me is: what have you done for me lately?"

That's how the world thinks. The world is interested in what is happening now. How you can help me now. What have you done for me lately? Jesus countered this fixation on the now with His statement to the rich farmer: "You fool! This very night your soul is required of you; and now who will own what you have prepared?" (Luke 12:20). We are to put off the wrong thinking which focuses on the temporary.

Paul Powell suggests three philosophies which encompass the thinking of the world: hedonism, materialism, and humanism. Hedonism proposes pleasure as the primary focus in life. Materialism exalts things as the chief value in life. Humanism concludes mankind is the central figure in life.[3] These philosophies grow out of the world's focus on the self, on the material, and on the temporary. As new creatures in Christ, we are to put off this wrong thinking.

Wrong Feeling (4:18-19)

The problem with the old self goes beyond our thinking and also includes our feeling. The old self not only produces wrong thinking. It also leads to wrong feeling. Paul described ones without Christ as those who suffer "the hardness of their heart" (v. 18) and have thus "become callous" (v. 19). The word "callous" *(apelgekotes)* means to be past feeling. Because the person without Christ thinks only on material and temporal things and because his thoughts are only on himself, his heart becomes hardened toward others, and he is no longer able to feel compassion for them.

A young man who served as pastor of a small rural church spent the summer working in the slums of Chicago. When he returned to his congregation in the fall, he shared his experiences and described the pain he felt over what he had seen. After the service, a retiree who had once lived in Chicago, said to the young pastor, "Don't worry about it, John. You'll get to the place where that sort of thing won't bother you anymore."[4] That is the way of the world. Many in the world have become hardened to the pain and suffering around them. The Christian is to put off that wrong kind of feeling. Instead, we are to feel compassion. What are the characteristics of Christian compassion?

Sensitivity.—A story in the Talmud describes three rabbis discussing how one can tell when dawn has arrived. One rabbi said, "It is dawn when you can tell a dog from a wolf." The second said, "It is dawn when you can distinguish blue thread from gold cloth." The third rabbi replied, "You know dawn has arrived when you are able to see your brother." The third rabbi was right. The sign that dawn has arrived, the keynote of Christian commitment, is the ability to see our brother as God sees him.[5] Because Christians are sensitive to those around them, they feel compassion.

Individuality.—Mother Teresa of Calcutta, the woman who ministers to the poor of her city, was asked one time how she keeps from being overwhelmed by the masses of the needy. She replied, "I love them one at a time." Because Christians see every individual as being important to God, they feel compassion.

Genuineness.—Two golfers were putting out on the ninth green when a funeral procession drove by. One of the men stopped, took off his hat and put it over his heart, and stood at attention until the procession had gone by. His partner said, "I am really impressed by your compassion for that dead person." "Yes," said the first man, "If she had lived until next month, we would have been married thirty years!" Like the man in that facetious story, we often fake our concern for others. Christian compassion is genuine. Because Christians recognize the hurts in other peoples' lives, they feel compassion.

An ancient story tells of a beggar who came to Moses and asked for bread. Moses invited him into his tent. Moses set out food before them. Before he ate, Moses offered praise to God. The beggar watched in silence as Moses expressed his praise. Moses asked the newcomer, "Why did you not praise God?" The beggar responded, "Why should I praise God? What has He done for me?" Moses, angry at the man's remarks, beat the man, and chased him out of his tent. When the beggar had gone, God said to Moses, "Why did you not feed the beggar?" Moses responded in self-righteousness, "Because he did not praise You." God answered, "Moses, that man has not praised Me for twenty years, and I have not destroyed him. The reason he has not praised Me is that you have neglected him. He is alive at all only because I am less religious than you are and have not destroyed him. If I were as religious as you appear to be, there would be no one left alive on the earth!"[6]

Condemnation and criticism grow out of the world's focus on self. As new creatures in Christ, we are to put off that wrong feeling.

Wrong Acting (4:19-21)

This wrong thinking and wrong feeling lead to wrong acting. Because the person without Christ is confused in his thinking and calloused in his feeling, he gives himself to a life described with two words.

Unrestrained

The person without Christ gives himself to a life of "sensuality" (v. 19). This word *(aselegia)* means "unbridled lust." The word describes the complete surrender of self. This is a person who lives under no restraints at all. The person without Christ also gives himself to a life of impurity (v. 19). This word *(akatharsias)* describes moral uncleanness in the broadest sense of that word. This is a person who involves himself in every kind of immorality imaginable.

A man sat down in the doctor's office and described a chronic digestion problem. The doctor asked about any situation causing undue stress in his life. "Yes," the man said, "I am married, but I am having an affair with a girlfriend in Syracuse. Twice a week I drive my old pickup down to see her. Since the pickup frequently breaks down, I am often late arriving at home. Consequently, I have to devise incredible stories to tell my wife. That puts me under a lot of stress." The doctor told the man he needed to make a hard decision about his personal priorities if he was to ever become well. Six months later the doctor bumped into this man and discovered he was over his digestion problem. The doctor congratulated him and delicately inquired if he had made a change in his life. "Yes," the man responded, "I bought a new pickup I could depend on!"

That's the way the world acts. The man never considered living within the restraints of his marriage relationship. He refused to live under any restraints at all. As new creatures in Christ, we are to put off that wrong kind of acting.

Unsatisfied

What is the motivation for this unrestrained, immoral way of acting? Paul explained with the word "greediness." This word *(pleonexia)* describes a person who always wants more. No matter what he has, he is not satisfied.

Tolstoy described this way of acting in his story of the Russian peasant who was told he could have all the land he could walk around in the time between sunup and sundown. As soon as the sun broke across the horizon, the peasant started walking. About half way through the morning, he quickened his pace. He did not take time to eat lunch. He needed to keep walking. As the sun moved across the sky, this man moved quickly across the land, saying to himself as he went along, *This is mine. This is mine.* As the day came to a close, he realized he had only a short time to make it back to the starting point. He began running, sweat dripping from his fast-moving body. His heart was pounding as he strained his body toward the starting point. As he approached the spot he needed to reach, the sun was setting. He took a few more quick steps before he fell on his face, just short of the starting point. He was dead.

That's what drives the world—the desire for more: more money, more pleasure, more power, more things. As new creatures in Christ, we are to put off that wrong acting.

Conclusion

One of the history's greatest baseball players was Rogers Hornsby. He had a lifetime average of .358, second only to Ty Cobb's. He hit more than three hundred home runs in his career. In his 1924 season with the Cardinals, Hornsby batted .424. What was the secret of his success? He had natural talent, of course. Yet, what distinguished him from others was his discipline. He never went to see a movie because he was convinced it would hurt his batting eye. He didn't smoke, he didn't drink, he didn't stay up late, and the only thing he read in the paper was the box scores. He said, "Baseball is my life, the only think I know and can talk about, my only interest."[7]

If Hornsby was willing to put out of his life anything which would keep him from being a successful baseball player, we should be willing to put out of our life anything which will keep us from being an effective Christian. Paul instructed us where to begin. We are to put off the old self with its wrong thinking, its wrong feeling, and its wrong acting.

For Discussion

1. How is the difference in the Christian to be demonstrated?

2. What is the most crucial difference between the way the world thinks and the way a Christian thinks?

3. How can we combat the materialism of our day?

4. What are some characteristics of Christian compassion?

5. Why are those without Christ unsatisfied?

9 | A Better Way to Live

Ephesians 4:23-32

She was considered the richest woman in the world in the late nineteenth century. Yet, she looked like anything but a rich woman. She scurried around New York's financial district wearing a moth-eaten cape and a frayed bonnet, carrying a little sack which contained the unwrapped food for her lunch. She conducted her business with smudged hands and face. She sat on the floor of her office and shuffled her bonds and mortgage notes. She spent years living in tawdry boarding houses. At her death in 1916, it was estimated that she owned eight thousand parcels of land and she left an estate of more than $125 million. Her name was Hetty Green.[2] When we hear her story we realize she could have lived better. Because she had unlimited wealth at her disposal, she did not have to live in poverty.

We see many spiritual parallels to Hetty Green in the church today, Christians who put off the old self but who never put on the new self. Such Christians never claim their rightful inheritance as children of God. Paul said there is a better way to live. He described this better way in the closing verses of chapter 4. Paul delineated five dynamics of our new life in Christ. In each case, Paul presented the negative and the positive as well as the motivation.

Live with Truth Instead of Dishonesty (4:25)

An article in *Time* revealed the rampant dishonesty in America today. A study of resumes in the job market revealed 22 percent contained outright lies. Misrepresentation of job responsibilities, deception about job termination, upgrading degrees received, and claiming false degrees—all of these are common in job resumes today.[3] Deception has become a way of life in America. Paul said there is a better way to live, to live with truth instead of dishonesty.

The Negative

Paul began with the negative. "Laying aside falsehood" (v. 25) is the prelude to donning the truth. Falsehood stands in opposition to God's plan and purpose. Therefore, we are to lay it aside. The word "lay aside" *(apothemnoi)* was used of a man taking off his old, dirty clothes. As I waited for my son at baseball practice one afternoon, I noticed a child playing next to the baseball field. A big puddle of water remained from a rain earlier in the day. I watched the child head for the puddle and, before his mother could stop him, he fell face first into the puddle. She held him up by one arm and stripped his clothes off of him. That is the picture Paul painted in our text.

The tense of the verb is aorist which means an action completed in the past. Literally, it means, "Having put off once for all the lie." It is not something to contemplate at each juncture of our lives. It is something that is settled the moment we choose to follow Christ. Because He is the truth, we once for all turn our backs on lying as an acceptable practice.

The Positive

Refraining from falsehood opens the door to speaking the truth. People perpetrate two kinds of lies: a lie in speech and a lie in silence. We stifle the truth as much by our silence as by our falsehoods. We sin as much by refusing to speak the truth as by speaking untruth. That is why refraining from lying is not enough. We must also speak the truth.

When our children do something that will hurt them, we do not need to be silent. We need to speak the truth. When our relationship with our spouse seems to be losing some of its zest, we do not need to be silent. We need to speak the truth. When an injustice is being done, we do not need to be silent. We need to speak the truth. Our new life in Christ demands a positive commitment to speak the truth.

The Motivation

Why should we avoid falsehood and speak the truth? We are to avoid falsehood and embrace truth because "we are members of one another" (v. 25). Paul pictured the church as the body of Christ. A healthy body and a healthy church must follow the same pattern.

To have a healthy body, each part must send true readings to the other parts. What if our stomach was hungry but sent the message to the head that it was not hungry? The stomach would not be fed. What if the brain told our right foot to go to the right and our left foot to go to the left? We would be in a fix. What if our hand sent the message to the brain that a fire was not hot but cool and the hand was stuck into the fire? We would have a problem.

That is a picture of what will happen to the body of Christ if we deal falsely with each other. The healthy working of the body of Christ demands we deal honestly with each other for we are members of one another.

Live with Control Instead of Anger (4:26-27)

As the man drove down the road, another car tried to cut in front of him. He became extremely angry and was determined to get even. He pulled up behind the other car, so the other car sped up. He pulled up behind him again, and the other car sped up again. Finally, they were driving at such a high rate of speed that the man who wanted to get even lost control of his car. It overturned and rolled over four women who were walking along the shoulder of the road. Three of the women were killed! That is a picture of the high price of anger. Paul said there is a better way to live, with control instead of anger.

The Negative

Paul began with the negative. What did he mean when he said, "Be angry, and yet do not sin" (v. 26)? What did Paul mean? Two Greek words, both translated with our English word "anger," present contrasting emotions. *Thumos* speaks of a turbulent, passionate outburst. *Orge* speaks of an abiding and settled habit of mind which is aroused under certain conditions. Paul had *orge* in mind when he said, "Be angry." We Christians are to have an abiding, settled attitude of righteous indignation against sin and sinful things. That is all right. That is acceptable. That is what we should have. However, we are not to have the kind of anger which is aroused by personal irritation, the kind of anger which causes us to be exasperated, the kind of anger which smolders into personal resentment toward others. As a further word of caution, Paul said, "Yet do not sin." We should not allow that sense of righteous indignation to lead us into actions which dishonor God. Paul's negative admonition concerning anger relates to improper motive and inappropriate manifestation.

The Positive

Acceptable Christian anger is based on the proper motive and is expressed in the appropriate way. When Paul said "be angry" he was talking about anger over unrighteousness. Indignation when God's work is being hindered and God's word is being maligned and God's people are being hurt is proper in the life of a Christian.

Sometimes, however, our anger arises from improper motives. When that happens, Paul said, our anger is not to be held in but is to be manifest in healthy, acceptable ways, and we are to do it immediately. Paul said not to "let the sun go down on your anger" (v. 26). Yet another word for "anger" is used here *(parorgismo)* which speaks of an anger mingled with irritation and embitterment. When we allow that sense of anger to remain in our heart for too long, when we allow it to be mingled with irritation and embitterment, then it is wrong. So Paul said, "Do not let the sun go down on your anger."

The Motivation

Why should we refrain from sinning with our righteous indignation? Why should we not let the sun go down on our wrath? We are not to "give the devil an opportunity" (v. 27).

When we refuse to speak out against evil, when we do not react toward sin in the proper way, we are giving the devil an opportunity to spread his opposition to the work of God. On the other hand, when we become embittered toward others and harbor this kind of anger in our heart, we are also giving Satan an opportunity. An unhealed breach, an unreconciled quarrel, a grudge nourished in the heart of a believer, is a magnificent opportunity for the devil to sow dissension and discord among the people of God. By not properly handling our anger, we allow Satan to use our anger to bring despair to our own lives, dishonor to God, discouragement to others, and disunity to the body of Christ.

Live with Compassion Instead of Selfishness (4:28)

The movie *Amadeus* focused on the ambition and envy court composer Antonio Salieri had toward the brash but brilliant young musician Wolfgang Mozart. According to this movie, Salieri wanted to be a famous musician but did not have the talent level to reach that goal. Instead of developing the talent he did have, Salieri became obsessed with destroying the gifted musician, Mozart, who was drawing attention away from him. In the end, Mozart died and Salieri lost his mind. Both were victims of Salieri's envy. Paul said there is a better way to live, with compassion instead of selfishness.

The Negative

Stealing is to be excluded from the Christian life. Paul said, "Let him who steals steal no longer" (v. 28). To steal is to take something that is not ours and claim it for our own. Stealing is rampant in our country today.

Burglary.—Burglary is the most common kind of thievery. Every eighty-two seconds a robbery occurs in the United States. Every thirty seconds an automobile is stolen.

Shoplifting.—A more sophisticated kind of burglary is shoplifting. Last year, retailers lost more than $7 billion to shoplifters.

Inventory shrinkage.—Another form of burglary is inventory shrinkage caused by employees who steal from their employer. Some authorities estimate another $6 billion per year is lost to employees who steal from their companies. An estimated 40 percent of all employees are guilty of this form of burglary.

Time thieves.—Stealing time from our employers is another kind of thievery. Long lunches, excessive personal phone calls, constant socializing with workers, inattention to the job, falsely calling in sick—all of these forms of thievery cost businesses about $60 million a year.

Stealing in whatever form means to take something that is not ours and claim it for our own. Taking what does not belong to us, in whatever form, is unacceptable as a part of the life-style of the Christian. It was a part of the old self we need to put off.

The Positive

If we are not to steal things from others, how are we to obtain the things we need? Each Christian is to "labor, performing with his own hands what is good" (v. 28). That's how we are to obtain the things we need for life. We are to work for them.

Some go to the extremes in the matter of their work. Some are so lazy they do nothing. Like the housewife who was told by a vacuum cleaner salesman his machine would cut her housework in half and she said, "Good, I'll take two of them!" Others go to the extreme of working all the time. Like the wife who was so organized that whenever her husband got up to go to the bathroom in the middle of the night, she made up the bed!

The New Testament avoids the extremes of the sluggard who does not work at all and the workaholic who does nothing but work. The New Testament affirms work is not the ultimate value in life but is nevertheless something which is intrinsically good. Whatever our job, whatever our position, whatever our responsibility, we are to do it to the best of our ability.

The Motivation

The way to obtain material possession is not to steal from others but to work for them yourself. But why? The answer we would expect is, "In order that each person can provide for his own needs." However, that is not what Paul said. Paul said a person is to refrain from stealing and instead commit himself to his work "in order that he may have something to share with him who has need" (v. 28).

Paul presented the basic New Testament principle in relationship to the things of life: the principle of stewardship. God owns everything we have. He has made us managers of a part of it. In managing this trust, our primary motive is not to get but to give. Stealing means more than just taking what belongs to others and claiming it as our own. Stealing means taking what belongs to God and claiming it as our own. Stealing means taking hold of the good stuff of this world and doing with it as we please, regardless of the desire of God or the needs of others. That way of living does not belong in the life of a Christian.

Live with Encouragement Instead of Criticism (4:29)

Johnny did not like wearing ties and did not even own one. However, his new job required him to wear a tie each day so his mother bought two ties which he could wear on alternating days. The next time he ate with his mother he decided to wear one of the ties in her honor. When she saw him, she said, "Why don't you like the other tie?" Some people live like that: always critical, always looking for the worst in others. Paul said there was a better way to live, with encouragement instead of criticism.

The Negative

What comes out of our mouths can create problems for us and for others. So Paul said: "Let no unwholesome word proceed from your mouth" (v. 29). The word "unwholesome" *(sapros)* means corrupt or worthless. The word is used six other times in the New Testament and in each case it refers to rotten fruit that cannot be eaten. The construction of the sentence is actually: "every word that is corrupt, out of your mouth let it not proceed." The Greek word *pas* means every. This is an inclusive command which includes every word we say. What is unwholesome speech?

Vulgarity.—I visited once with a lady whose father had just died. In his last years, she told me, he had begun to say words she had never heard him say before. The lady's son, sitting with us, interrupted with this comment, "Well, I heard him say them plenty of times. He just never said them around you." The lady's image of her dead father was spoiled by the unwholesome words which proceeded from his mouth.

Criticism.—The power of our words to destroy others has been illustrated throughout history. Nowhere is that more evident than in the home. Family experts suggest our words will determine to a large degree the self-image of our children. When we constantly tell our children they are bad, they will probably become bad. When we constantly tell our children they are special, that image will shape their activities.

Triviality.—Perhaps the greatest sin of the tongue is that of the 30,000 words in the vocabulary of most college graduates, we use so few of them to speak of subjects of importance, so few of them to talk about spiritual matters, so few of them to talk about God.

Unacceptable words, unkind words, and unimportant words are a part of the misuse of the tongue which affects all of us today. That's why the prayer of the psalmist should be adopted by each of us today: "Set a watch, O Lord, before my mouth; keep the door of my lips" (Ps. 141:3, KJV). Because we are new creatures in Christ Jesus, we are not to allow unwholesome words to proceed out of our mouths.

The Positive

What kind of speech should we use? Paul explained: "only such a word as is good for edification according to the need of the moment" (v. 29). The word "edification" *(oikodomen)* means to build up. We are to use words that build people up, words that encourage.

In our homes.—We need words of encouragement in our homes. How important it is to speak to our children with the vocabulary of affirmation.

In our marriages.—We need words of encouragement in our marriages. One husband said about his wife, "She makes me feel good about myself with a pat high on the ego!" Say what you will about that marriage, it will grow.

In our churches.—We need words of encouragement in our churches. We need to remember Jesus did not come to condemn sinners but to seek and save those who are lost. Not judgment but grace, not condemnation but acceptance is the keynote of the gospel and must be the character of the church.

Maybe once in a hundred years a person can be ruined by excessive praise. Probably every minute someone dies from lack of it. We need to speak words that encourage, build up, and edify.

The Motivation

Why should we refuse to let unwholesome words come out of our mouths, and why should we speak only such words as are good for building up? Paul suggested this motivation: "that it may give grace to those who hear" (v. 29). Our main purpose is to be a channel through which the grace of God can touch the life of someone else. We are His representatives in the world. Every aspect of our lives—even the words we speak—are to be instruments by which the grace of God is communicated to others.

A little boy was leaning against the outside wall of a store one Christmas season. His whole body was shivering. A woman walked up to him and put her arms around him. "Are you cold?" she asked the little boy. He responded, "I was, till you spoke to me!" We need to warm up the world with words of encouragement as we allow the love of God to flow through our lives.

Live with Commitment Instead of Disobedience (4:30-32)

The mother was obviously at the end of her rope with her precocious three-year-old child. Every time the mother told her child to do something, the child did just the opposite. Finally, the frustrated mother told her three-year-old, "Do anything you want to do. Now, let's see you disobey that!" Some people seem to go through life doing exactly what they want to do, regardless of their responsibility to others or their responsibility to God. Paul said there is a better way to live, with commitment instead of disobedience.

The Negative

To every believer God gives the Holy Spirit. However, in some Christians the Holy Spirit has the freedom to do His work while in others, He is hindered. As Paul explained, some Christians "grieve the Holy Spirit of God, by whom you were sealed for the day of redemption" (v. 30). The Holy Spirit is the spiritual presence of God dwelling in the heart of every believer. However, it is possible to grieve the Holy Spirit who lives within our lives. How do we grieve the Holy Spirit?

Bitterness.—We grieve the Holy Spirit with our "bitterness" (v. 31). This Greek word *(pikria)* means the kind of resentment that refuses to be reconciled. It means harshness or resentfulness. An example is a family I ministered to several years ago. A daughter in the family decided to marry a young man who did not meet the approval of an older sister. The older sister turned her back on the one getting married. She would not be

with her. She refused to go to the wedding. More than a year passed
before she would even talk to her. Another sister, who filled me in on the
details of the story, shared how this almost destroyed her parents with
grief. Resentment between brothers in Christ which we refuse to recon-
cile causes the same kind of grief in the heart of God.

Anger.—We grieve the Holy Spirit with our "anger," both the kind
that erupts into violent expression *(thumos)* and the kind that simmers
over a long period of time, *(orge)* (v. 31). When expressed, this anger
causes clamor in the family of faith. The word clamor *(krauge)* refers to
the outward manifestation of anger in fighting. Expressions of anger between those of us who are supposed to be brothers, which causes us to
fight with one another instead of love one another, grieves the Holy
Spirit. What grieves the Holy Spirit is Christians who share a common
faith, who are brothers in Christ, who are part of the body of Christ, who
will not get along with each other.

Slander.—We grieve the Holy Spirit with our "slander" (v. 31). Un-
true or unkind statements about our fellow Christians bring sorrow to
the heart of God. We often make jokes about it, like the girl who said to a
friend, "I make it a habit never to say anything about anyone unless it is
good. And, boy, is this good!" However, it is no laughing matter to God.
Instead, our slander of others discredits our witness and dishonors our
God.

The Positive

Instead of being angry with each other, we are to reach out in kindness. Paul said, "Be kind to one another, tender-hearted, forgiving each
other" (v. 32). This is how we are to relate to one another in the body of
Christ. When we treat each other with loving-kindness *(krestoi)*, when
we are "tender-hearted" *(eusplagchnoi)* to each other, when we are willing to treat others as if they had done us no harm *(charizomenoi)*, we
bring joy to the heart of God.

The Talmud refers to ten strong things. Iron is strong, but fire melts it.
Fire is strong, but water quenches it. Water is strong, but the clouds
evaporate it. Clouds are strong, but the wind drives them away. Man is
strong, but fears cast him down. Fear is strong, but sleep overcomes it.
Sleep is strong, yet death is stronger. But loving-kindness survives
death.[4]

When we treat each other with loving kindness, when we are tender-
hearted to each other, when we are willing to forgive, we are not only
putting into effect life's strongest force, but we are also bringing joy to
the heart of God.

The Motivation

Why should we put out of our lives bitterness, anger, clamor, and slander? Why should we treat one another with kindness, tenderness, and forgiveness? This is the motivation: Just as God in Christ has also forgiven you" (v. 32). We love others because God first loved us.

God set a pattern for kindness, for the Bible says, "But God demonstrates His own love toward us, in that while we were yet sinners, Christ died for us" (Rom. 5:8). God set a pattern for forgiveness when on the cross Christ said, "Father, forgive them, for they know not what they do"(Luke 23:34, KJV). We are to follow His pattern. If you want to bring joy to the Holy Spirit instead of grieving the Holy Spirit you can do it by the way you relate to others.

Conclusion

Adoniram Judson and his wife Ann were pioneer missionaries to Burma. Adoniram was characterized by a sweet spirit and a deep commitment to God. One day, Ann read a newspaper clipping of their work. She read a statement in the article which compared Judson to one of the apostles. He was not amused by the comparison but rather he was bothered by it. He explained, "I do not want to be like them. I want to be like Christ!"[5] Jesus is the model and pattern for our new life. When we live like Him, we have discovered a better way to live.

For Discussion

1. Why do so many Christians live beneath their privileges?

2. What can we do in the church to increase the commitment to honesty?

3. Is anger always wrong for the Christian? If not, why not?

4. Why is it easier to be critical than encouraging? What steps can we take to become better encouragers?

5. In what ways do we grieve the Holy Spirit?

10 Learning How to Walk

Ephesians 5:1-21

As a parent of four children, I have a lot of memories. One of the most vivid and exciting memories is the moment our first son, Jay, walked for the first time. I remember when it happened. I remember where Jan and I were. I can even feel the excitement we felt as Jay took those first steps. Nothing thrills a parent more than for the child to learn how to walk. Our Heavenly Father must feel the same thing as we learn to walk as Christians. In this chapter, Paul described the Christian walk.

Walk in Love (5:1-2)

Paul began chapter 5 with one of the most incredible statements in any of his epistles. Paul challenged us to "be imitators of God" (v. 1). We get our word *mimic* from the Greek word *imitators (mimetai)*. We are to mimic God. We are to try to be like God. What did Paul mean? Paul clarified his point in verse 2. We are to imitate God by walking in love. In other words, we are to be like God in His love.

This is not the only place in the Scripture where we are challenged to love like God. We see the same thought in 1 John 4:11: "Beloved, if God so loved us, we also ought to love one another." Likewise, in Luke 6:35, Jesus said, "But love your enemies . . . and you will be sons of the Most High; for He Himself is kind to ungrateful and evil men." The New Testament frequently presents this challenge to imitate God's love.

Paul changed the imagery slightly in verse 2 when he said we are to "walk in love" (v. 2). The word *walk (peripateite)* refers to the way we live our lives, the attitude which characterizes our everyday lives. Our walk, as the word is used in the New Testament, includes our thoughts, our words, and our deeds. Everything we think, everything we say, and everything we do is to be characterized by love.

How Can We Walk in Love?

How can we imitate the love of God? How can we walk in that same kind of love? Paul presented two motivations.

Because of who we are (v. 1).—We are to be imitators of God "as be-loved children." Children have a unique capacity to mimic. Many of the first things they do as babies they copy from their parents. Some of the first words they say are words they hear their parents say.

One youngster said several words that were unacceptable to his moth-er, so she sent him to his room. When the father came home, she told him what his son had said. The father was furious. "I'll teach that boy to curse," the father said as he stormed up the steps to punish him. On the way up the steps, the father stepped on a roller skate which had been inadvertently left on the steps. As the father tumbled down the steps he let out one expletive after another. Finally, when he got to the bottom of the steps and stood up, his wife said to him, "Honey, I think that's enough for his first lesson!"

Children naturally imitate their fathers and mothers. Have you ever seen a little child trying to drive like his mother or dad? Have you ever seen a little child trying to walk like his mother or dad? We are children of God. We have been adopted into His forever family. He is our Father. Because of that, we should be able to imitate Him.

Because of what Christ has done (v. 2).—We ought to be able to imitate God's love because of the model and motivation Jesus gave to us on the cross. We are to "walk in love, just as Christ also loved you, and gave Himself up for us, an offering and a sacrifice to God as a fragrant aroma" (v. 2).

We use the word *love* in a multitude of different ways today. Some things we label with the word *love* are not love at all. What is love? Jesus showed us what love is. Christ loved us, and gave Himself up for us freely and sacrificially. He gave Himself as an offering. That is, He freely gave Himself. He gave Himself as a sacrifice. That is, He gave all of Himself. That's what love is. It is a purposeful, willing, self-sacrificing concern for others in which we give ourselves to them. When we follow Christ's ex-ample and deliberately adopt a life-style which focuses more on what we can do for others than on what we can obtain for ourselves, then we will be able to walk in love.

What Does It Mean to Walk in Love?

To walk in love means to imitate the kind of love God demonstrated for us. This means to give and to forgive.

To give.—John 3:16 begins with the words: "God so loved the world, that He gave." That is a description of what God has always done. He has always given. In Genesis, He gave life. In Exodus, He gave the law.

In Joshua, He gave the land. In the Psalms, He gave strength and comfort. In the Gospels, He gave His Son. In Acts, He gave the Holy Spirit. In Revelation, He gave hope. It is God's nature to give. That is the heart of His love. To imitate God in our walk of love means our lives are to be characterized by a giving spirit toward others.

To forgive.—Paul referred in verse 2 to Jesus' death as being "a sacrifice to God." The purpose of a sacrifice was to atone for man's sin and obtain forgiveness. The purpose in Christ's giving Himself for us was that He might obtain forgiveness for us.

This is another dimension of God's love. God's love is not only a giving kind of love. God's love is also a forgiving kind of love. One of the most beautiful expressions of forgiving love was the amazing story of the conversion of the Auca Indians in South America. In January 1956 five young American missionaries were killed by these Indians. Today, the five living Auca killers are all Christians, leaders of the small congregation which worships near the spot where the missionaries died. The thatched Auca church, called "God's speaking-house," was built by the five killers. How did this radical transformation come about? Because Rachel Saint, sister of martyred Nate Saint, and Betty Elliot, wife of the martyred Jim Elliot, went back to these people who had killed their loved ones and demonstrated in their walk of love the reality of forgiveness. If God is able to forgive us for our sins, if those ladies were able to forgive the atrocities against their loved ones, then we need to forgive those who have hurt us. That's what love means. It means the willingness to forgive.

Walk in Light (5:3-14)

To walk as a Christian also means to walk in light. Two questions focus our attention on this challenge: "What does it mean to walk in light?" and "Why then should we do that?"

What Does It Mean to Walk in Light?

In verse 3, Paul gave a number of different words which should not characterize the life of a Christian. All of these words are associated with darkness. These are the things we need to put out of our lives in order for us to walk in the light.

Immorality (v. 3).—Our word *pornography* comes from the word translated *immorality (porneia)*. The word means illicit sexual relationships in general. Specifically, the word refers to sexual permissiveness. Paul described the kind of life with no barriers or restrictions to the expression of our sexuality. Paul said, "That is the way it is with those who walk in the darkness. But those who walk in the light are not to allow that kind of immorality to be in their life"(author's words). To walk in light means our sexuality is to be expressed within the context God intended: between a husband and a wife who have made a permanent commitment to each other. To walk in light means to control the sexual dimension of life which is the opposite of immorality. To walk in light includes control.

Impurity (v. 3).—The Greek word for *impurity (akatharsia)* is a more general word than the previous word. This word refers to immorality in a broader sense. This word is often used in the New Testament to refer to someone who is sick and unclean. Many of those who Jesus healed were considered *akatharsia* They were unclean. Such an illness permeated the whole life. Paul said, "Those who are in darkness not only are having problems in the sexual dimension of life, but also as a general rule are immoral in all of the different dimensions of their life. Those who walk in light are not to allow that in their life" (author's words). Those who are in the light are those who live a clean life. To walk in light includes cleanliness.

Greed (5:3).—The word *greed (pleonexia)* literally means "overreaching." The word described somebody who has something but is not satisfied with that, so he reaches over to somebody else.

Consider little children. Do you know what we noticed when our children were little? We would get a toy for one child and a toy for another. Do you know what they would do after a few seconds? Each one would want the toy the other one had. The word *greed* paints the picture of a person who has something but is never satisfied with it. This person is always reaching over to someone else's possessions and trying to draw these to themselves.

The opposite of greed is contentment. To walk in light means to face life with the attitude Paul had when he said, "I have learned to be content in whatever circumstances I am" (Phil. 4:11). Contentment does not mean to come to the point in our life where we say, "I am all I need to be and I have all I need in life." Contentment instead is the recognition that what we have is a gift from God and what we are is a result of the grace of God, and we are therefore content with what God has done for us up to that point. To walk in light includes contentment.

Filthiness (v. 4).—The word for *filthiness (aischrotes)* carries with it the idea of obscene thinking or shameless thinking. Paul's concern was with the focus of our minds, the things to which we give attention. Paul said, "Those in darkness concentrate on what is obscene, what is immoral, what is bad" (author's words). In contrast, to walk in light means to concentrate on those things that are good, those things that are right. A person who walks in light concentrates on good, positive, godly things. To walk in light includes concentration.

Silly talk (v. 4).—The Greek word for "silly talk" *(morologia)* comes from two words. The word *logia* refers to words and we get *moron* from *moro*. Paul was talking about a foolish kind of speaking. Paul said, "Those in darkness talk foolishly" (author's words). In contrast, to walk in light means not to speak foolishly.

What is foolish speaking? It is talking without foresight. Many times, we say things without thinking through what we are going to say. We say things we do not really mean. We say things we wish we had not said. Foolish speaking is also talking without wisdom. Not only do we not think about the ultimate result of what we said. On many occasions, we do not think through what we were going to say to make sure we say it the right way. Words void of foresight and void of wisdom ought not to be in the life of the Christian. To walk in light means to think about what we are going to say, to think about the consequences of what we say. To walk in light includes carefulness.

Coarse jesting (v. 4).—The word translated "coarse jesting" is a very interesting word, with a different meaning from what we would think at first glance. We think of a jester as someone who is always telling jokes, a happy-go-lucky kind of guy. That is not what this word means. Paul's word *(eutrapelia)* is made of two words which mean to turn easily. The picture is of a person in one crowd which is telling bad jokes, so he tells bad jokes. Then he comes to a crowd at church which is singing praises, so he sings praises. Then he goes with a group which is criticizing, so he criticizes. He turns easily. He adjusts to the crowd he is with. Some adjusting is good. However, the kind of adjusting Paul was talking about is not good. Such a person is shaped by circumstances rather than by inner commitment.

Paul said, "Those who walk in the darkness are like that. They are always trying to find their crowd. They are always wanting to be popular. They are always wanting everybody to like them, so whatever crowd they are in, they just turn easily to fit in with that crowd. That is not what a person who walks in the light is supposed to do. A person who walks in the light is to base his behavior not on his outward circumstances but on his inward commitment" (author's words). To walk in light means to consistently live out of this inner commitment. To walk in light includes consistency.

Idolatry (v. 5).—Idolatry means to worship an idol, to worship something other than God. All of us constantly face the temptation to give our commitment to something other than God. Every day we face that challenge. Sometimes, even our family can become an idol. Sometimes our job can become an idol. Sometimes money can become an idol. Sometimes our own desires can become an idol. Putting anything above God is idolatry. Those who walk in light are to be committed to God. He is to be our top priority. To walk in light includes commitment.

Why Should We Walk in the Light?

Why should we live this kind of life? Paul provided three motives in our text.

The identity motive (v. 3).—The word *saint (hagiosis)* is one of the important words of the New Testament. Unfortunately, we have distorted the word and given it a bad connotation. We move from saint to sanctimonious which pictures a person who is so spiritual he thinks he is better than everyone else. In its biblical usage, a saint is simply one set aside for a special kind of life.

We should walk in light because we have been set aside for a specific kind of life. In the ancient world, immorality was common. An immoral life-style was the standard way of living in the ancient world. Into that ancient world came Jesus Christ who introduced a new way of living, a new understanding of life, a new commitment to morality. He called His followers to exhibit this new life-style. Therefore, when we walk in the light, we are identifying with the people Jesus wants us to be.

The implementation motive (v. 9).—We are to walk in light because of what walking in the light does for us. Paul said, "For the fruit of the light consists in all goodness and righteousness and truth." This fruit, produced by the light, stands in contrast to the unfruitful deeds of darkness. Light always produces growth. Darkness always inhibits growth. This is true in the physical world. It is also true in the spiritual world. We ought to walk in the light because of what walking in the light will do for us. It will help us to grow into the kind of person God wants us to be.

The influence motive (v. 13).—We are to walk in light not only because of who we are, not only because of what it does for us, but also because of what it does for others. William Barclay translates verse 13: "And everything which is illuminated becomes light."[1] As we walk in light, it not only causes us to grow, but it causes us to throw off this glow. As this glow emanates from our lives, everything the light touches is influenced by it.

All of us know somebody like that. Just to be around that person influences us for the good. Just to be in that person's presence somehow makes us want to do things for the Lord. I have people like that in my life. I enjoy being around them because when I am around them their glow comes over on my life.

A college student, about to graduate, had gone through four years without darkening the doors of a church. He went to see the pastor of the church next to the college campus. He admitted, "I have ridiculed the church since I came to school. I have not gone to church. Not only that, I have made fun of those who did. I called them all kinds of names and did everything I could to make life miserable for them. But this year, my senior year, I realized I am soon to be out of here, and I am going to have to determine what my place in life is. I realized the direction I was going and the kind of life I was living was a dead-end street. I observed some who were members of this church. I played on intramural ball fields with them. I lived in apartments with them. I had classes with them. I watched the way they related. I watched everything about their lives, and I want to ask you this morning how I can experience in my life what they have." When we walk in light, our light will become a positive force which produces life in others.

Walk in Wisdom (5:15-21)

Another characteristic of our walk as Christians is wisdom. We are to walk "not as unwise men, but as wise" (v. 15). Paul used the same word twice. In the first instance, he preceded the word with the little letter *a*, the alpha privative, which is like our English prefix *un*. *Wise* is *sophos* *Unwise* is *asophos*. The Christian is to walk in wisdom *(sophos)* not in unwisdom *(asophos)*. This is another checkpoint for the Christian life. Are we walking as a Christian is supposed to walk? Ask the question: "Am I walking in wisdom?" What does it mean to walk in wisdom?

Redeem the Time (5:16)

The wise person makes the most of his time. The Greek word for making the most of *(exagorazomenoi)* means "to buy up." In the middle voice, as it is used here, it means "to buy up for one's self or for one's own advantage." It means to make the very best use of our time. The Greek word for time is not *chronos,* which is simply time as it passes but *kairos,* which refers to special time, strategic opportunities. Every day we have special opportunities which come our way, opportunities to make a difference for Christ, opportunities to speak a word for God, opportunities to grow in our Christian life, opportunities to meet someone else's need, opportunities to develop a relationship. The wise person takes advantage of those opportunities.

Notice the motivation Paul gave. We are to make the most of our time "because the days are evil." The word for "evil" *(ponerai)* means active opposition to the things of God. Every day, when the special opportunities for service come along, evil is actively at work, trying to turn those opportunities into something which will dishonor God and discredit God's word. We need to be just as alert, just as aggressive, just as in tune as evil is so we can turn those opportunities into something which will honor God and affirm His word.

Do God's Will (5:17)

The wise person also does God's will. "The will of the Lord" is a phrase which in one form or another permeates the Bible. God has certain things He wants to accomplish in the world. God has certain things He wants to achieve in our lives. God has certain laws He wants us to live by so we can get the most out of life. God has certain ways He wants us to relate to others. God has certain responses He wants us to make to the challenges and crises of life. All of those things can be summarized in the one phrase: the will of the Lord.

The wise Christian understands what the will of the Lord is. "Understand" *(sunientes)* means "to set or bring together." Understanding the will of the Lord comes when we bring our perception together with the will of God. How do we do that? How do we know what God wants to accomplish in the world, and what He wants us to achieve in us, and how He wants us to live, and how He wants us to relate, and how He wants us to respond? How do we know those things? God has revealed these things to us in His word.

Every day we have to make choices between doing God's will and doing our will, between doing what God wants and doing what the world suggests. When we consistently study God's Word so we know in our hearts what His will is, we are able, when the choices come to decide to do God's will.

Walk in the Spirit (5:18-21)

The Christian is able to walk in love, in light, and in wisdom when he walks in the Spirit. The Christian is not to live under the control of man-made intoxicants. Instead, he is to be under the control of the Spirit. In contrast to the physical stimulus that leads to riotousness, Paul urged a spiritual stimulus that leads to righteousness. We are to "be filled with the Spirit."

John R. W. Stott delineated four points in this challenge. The challenge is in the imperative mood. It is in the plural form. It is in the passive voice. It is in the present tense. The imperative mood means it is a command. The plural form means it is addressed to all those reading the epistle. The passive voice means the filling will be done to them. The present tense shows it is to be an ongoing experience.[2]

When we walk in the Spirit, several things will result.

Joy (5:19)

When a person walks in the Spirit he will be "speaking to one another in psalms and hymns and spiritual songs, singing and making melody with your heart to the Lord." Here, as in Galatians 5:22, Paul declared joy to be a fruit of the Spirit.

A television advertisement for comedy programs pictured a clergyman dressed in black with a reversed collar and a solemn expression on his face. The sign on the ad read, "Our programs can make anyone laugh." The implication was that a Christian does not know how to laugh, that religion and sadness are synonymous. The opposite is actually true. Real joy comes when a person is under the influence of the Holy Spirit, walking in harmony with the God who made him.

Thankfulness (5:20)

When a person walks in the Spirit, he will be "always giving thanks for all things in the name of our Lord Jesus Christ to God, even the Father." The words *thank* and *think* come from the same root word. As we think about what the Holy Spirit is doing in and through us, then we will thank God. When we come under the influence of the Holy Spirit we are in touch with the God who is adequate to meet our every challenge and sufficient enough to satisfy our every need and powerful enough to meet our every problem. That will make us thankful.

G. K. Chesterton said the saddest moment in the life of an atheist is when he realizes he has something for which to be thankful but no one to thank.[3] Not so with the person under the influence of the Holy Spirit. We not only have much for which to be thankful. We also have someone to thank.

Submission (5:21)

When persons walk in the Spirit, they will "be subject to one another in the fear of Christ." When we are under the influence of the Holy Spirit, self is removed from the center of our lives, and we are able to look at others through the eyes of Christ. The result is a willingness to submit to the needs and desires of others. When we do that, wonderful benefits will come.

This was beautifully illustrated in Spokane, Washington. During the winter, a man's car would never start. Repeatedly, he called on the help of the landlord who would jump-start his car. Then, one day in the following summer, the landlord's heart stopped and his wife called on the young tenant to help. This young man, who had been trained in CPR for ten years, jump-started his landlord's heart to save his life.[4]

As we submit to each other, we will not only reap positive benefits, but we will also be walking as God wants us to walk.

For Discussion

1. What does it mean to walk in love?
2. What are some things which should not be allowed in the life of a Christian?
3. What are three motives for walking in light?
4. How does wisdom manifest itself in the life of the Christian?
5. What results does the Spirit produce within the Christian?

11 | Being a Christian at Home

Ephesians 5:22 to 6:4

After her surgery, Julie was being cared for by her daughter, Pam. Pam brought Julie her dinner on a tray and straightened out the covers. Julie said, "It's funny. This is what I used to do for you when you were sick, and now you are taking care of me."

Pam responded, "We take turns."

That is a Christian home at its best, a place where we take turns helping each other. To accomplish that, each member of the family needs to recognize and fulfill his or her responsibility. Paul addressed these reciprocal responsibilities in his timeless discussion on the Christian family. Ray Summers has written of this passage: "It is scarcely possible to conceive of a nobler view of marriage and the home than that which appears in this passage in Ephesians."[1]

The Challenge to Wives (5:22-24)

In verse 22, Paul wrote the often-quoted admonition: "Wives, be subject to your own husbands, as to the Lord." Literally, the Greek says, "Wives to your own husbands." The word *subject* is not in the text in verse 22. It is supplied from verse 21. The phrase "as to the Lord" does not mean that the wife is to relate to her husband in the same way she relates to the Lord. Instead, it tells her how she is to relate to her husband because she is related to the Lord. She is to treat her own husband (v. 22) with the same spirit and the same attitude with which she relates to every person (v. 21). That is, a wife is to relate to her husband with a spirit of humility and respect.

Paul elaborated on that initial instruction in verses 23-24. The husband is to be "the head of the wife, as Christ also is the head of the church." Paul exalted the relationship between Christ and the church as the pattern for the relationship between the husband and his wife. What dimension of the relationship between Christ and His church is to be the pattern for the husband and wife? Paul added in the next phrase: "He Himself being the Savior of the body" (v. 23).

Does that phrase explain the preceding phrase or does it stand in contrast to it? Some see this phrase, "He Himself being the Savior of the body," as standing in contrast to the preceding phrase, "as Christ is the head of the church." In other words, they see this phrase as differentiating between the husband and Christ. In this case, the verse would be translated to say: "The husband is the head of the wife as Christ is the head of the church, only with this difference, Christ is also the Savior of the church, something the husband is not."

In the absence of any other indicators, the most natural interpretation of that phrase is to see it not as a contrast but as an explanation. In this case, the verse would be translated to say: "The husband is the head of the wife as Christ is the head of the church, in this way, as Christ gave Himself for the church as the church's Savior, even so the husband is to give of himself to protect and care for his wife." The second phrase explains in what way the husband's relationship with the wife can be compared with Christ's relationship with the church.

The wives are to relate to their husbands "as the church is subject to Christ" (v. 24). The Greek word connecting verses 23 and 24 is translated *but (alla)*. Most interpret it as a word of contrast as if to contrast verse 24 with verses 22-23. William Hendriksen concluded that the word *alla* is not to be understood as a word of contrast but as a word of summary. In other words, verse 24 summarized what Paul said in verses 22-23. It should be translated *then*.[2] Because Christ gave Himself for the church out of love and concern, the church needs to respond to Christ with humility and respect. Likewise, because the husband gives himself for his wife to protect her and care for her out of love and concern, the wife needs to respond to her husband with humility and respect.

Does this passage present a well-formulated pattern of order in the home which is taught under the headship theory, which suggests that the husband is to make the decisions in the home and the wife is to be submissive to and obedient to him? In making up your mind about this important issue, remember these thoughts. A careful exposition of the passage which we have just done, looking at the words themselves and not reading into them preconceived notions, does not support such a well-formulated theory. In addition, the same word is used in verse 21 to describe every Christian's attitude toward every other Christian which is used in verse 24 to speak of the wife's attitude toward her husband. The two usages of the word in such close proximity must be the same. If the word in verse 24 means the husband is the head of the wife in the sense of ruler, then the word in verse 21 means every Christian is to make every other Christian head over him in the sense of ruler. This would not make sense. Further, Paul's conclusion in verse 33 to this discussion on the duties of husband and wife summarizes their respective responsibilities in this way: "[a husband should] love his own wife even as himself; and let the wife see to it that she respect her husband."

So here is Paul's word for wives. Christian wives are not independent from their husbands, nor should they be self-assertive in relationship to their husbands. Rather, they are to carry over the Christian attitude into their home and treat their husbands with the same sense of respect and humility they display in relationship with everyone.

The Challenge to Husbands (5:25-33)

What about the husband? How is he supposed to relate to his wife? Paul explained beginning in verse 25. In that day, men were the dominant figures in the home. Wives were subject to their husbands and in fact had to be. In Paul's word to the Christian wives, he moved beyond the subject obedience which characterized all wives to opt for a kind of respect which would establish the husband/wife relationship on a higher level. An even more radical word was Paul's challenge to Christian husbands to love their wives. The present imperative speaks of continuous action. Husbands were to make a habit of loving their wives. How is a husband to love his wife? Paul described three characteristics of a husband's love.

A Sacrificing Love (5:25)

Paul challenged husbands to love their wives "just as Christ also loved the church and gave Himself up for her." The love Christ had for the church was a sacrificing love.

An accountant proposed to the girl of his dreams saying, "I'd like to make a joint income-tax return with you!" He was thinking more of what he could get from his wife than of what he could give to his wife. That is typical of many marriages today. The primary cause of the high divorce rate today is selfishness. Looking out for number one has become the basic philosophy of the nineties. Our love is usually a demanding love.

How different from the picture of love Paul painted in our text. Christ loved the church in such a way He "gave Himself up for her." Paul referred in Galatians 2:20 to Jesus "who loved me, and gave himself for me" (KJV). The beautiful gospel in a nutshell in John 3:16 begins, "For God so loved the world, that He gave . . . ."

One woman said her husband spoke three languages: golf, football, and baseball. When a husband really loves his wife, he will speak a fourth language—the language of sacrifice and self-giving.

A Sanctifying Love (5:26-27)

As Christ loved the church and sanctified it, a husband is to love his wife and sanctify her. "To sanctify" *(hagiasu)* means "to set apart for sacred use." The word carries the connotation of equipping and enabling our wives to be all they were meant to be. A husband is to help his wife become all God made her to be. That is how a husband shows his love.

The more I study how Jesus related to women and what He said about them, the more convinced I am that the revolutionary teaching He brought from God is that a woman's value is not to be seen in her relationships with her father, her husband, or her children. It is found in her own individuality as a unique person created by God with special gifts and a distinct destiny. A husband who loves his wife will help her discover who she really is, and will encourage her and enable her to become all God made her to be. He will love his wife with a sanctifying love.

A Satisfying Love (5:28-29)

As a man nourishes and cherishes his own body, so is he is to relate to his wife. The word *cherish (thalpei)* originally meant "to warm" but eventually came to mean "to foster with tender care." It means to bring a sense of satisfaction.

At the root of today's marital dilemma is the failure of husbands to love their wives enough to meet their needs. In fact, many husbands do not even love their wives enough to know what their needs are. A wife told her counselor what she wanted from her husband. She explained, "I would like for my husband to look me up first when he gets home, before he turns to his hobby. I would like for my husband to say he loved me in front of someone else. I would like for my husband to kiss me somewhere other than in bed." Discovering the needs of his wife is the first step for a husband to display a satisfying kind of love.

One lady advertised in a newspaper for a husband and she received scores of replies, all from women who said, "You can have mine!" These were wives whose husbands did not love them with a satisfying kind of love.

Paul summarized his message to husbands and wives in verse 33. Husbands are to love their wives. Wives are to respect their husbands. Christian marriages are to be different. This difference is to be reflected in the respect Christian wives have for their husbands and the love Christian husbands have for their wives.

The Challenge to Children (6:1)

Another crucial relationship in the home is the parent/child relationship. Paul addressed that subject beginning with the responsibility of the child.

A woman dialed the phone, intending to call a record store to order a new album. However, she dialed the wrong number. The man who answered was a plumber. Unaware of her mistake, the woman asked, "Do you have 'Eyes of Blue and a Heart That's True'?" "No," the plumber replied, "but I have a wife and eight children on Sunset Lane." The woman paused for a moment before responding, "Is that a record?" The plumber answered, "Well, I don't know, but it's way above average."

The average number of children in a family has greatly decreased in recent days. A new national organization for nonparents has even been formed. Yet, most married couples do have children. What is the responsibility of these children?

Obey (6:1)

Paul urged Christian children to "obey your parents in the Lord, for this is right" (v. 1). The word "obey" *(hupakouete)* literally means "to hear under" and implies that a child is to listen to his parents who have authority over him and then do what the parents say. The verb is in the present imperative which implies continuous action. Children are to continuously listen to their parents so they can do what they say. Why should a child obey his parents? Notice the two modifying phrases: "in the Lord" and "for this is right."

"*In the Lord*."—That phrase does not modify parents but rather it modifies obey. That is, children are to obey their parents not because their parents are "in the Lord" but because this is what the Lord wants them to do. As they obey their parents, they please the Lord. As they obey their parents they displease the Lord. They are to do it in the Lord.

"*For this is right*."—Obedience is the right thing for a child to do. The child owes his very existence to the parent. The parent has the experience with which to make a wiser decision. In addition, in normal situations, no one loves the child any more than the parents. Therefore, it is right for a child to obey his parents.

Honor (6:2)

The word "honor" *(tima)* means "to estimate" or "to fix the value." To honor our parents means to correctly estimate their value and to act accordingly. Honor is the inner attitude that leads to the outward action of obedience. This honor and respect are to be shown to both father and mother. Both parents are equal in stature and in importance in the home. The child is to respond to both of them with the same degree of respect.

Paul described this command to honor parents as "the first commandment with a promise" (v. 2). What did that mean? Many solutions are suggested, but the best seems to be translating verse 6 to say that the commandment to honor father and mother is "a commandment first with a promise." The first does not mean first in terms of its appearance but a commandment which is significant. Paul said the commandment to honor parents is a significant commandment and it is one that has a promise attached to it.

What is the promise? The promise is for a good life and a long life (v. 3). How is this promise to be understood?

Individually.—Obedience to parents is one of the factors determining the length of a person's life. Disobedience to parents indicates an undisciplined life which often results in vice and dissipation. Obedience to parents indicates a disciplined, controlled life which often results in goodness and growth. The way a child responds to parents is a mirror of the way he responds to life, and the way he responds to life is one of the most important factors in determining the quality of his life and the length of his life.

Collectively.—Some have applied the promise not to individuals but to the nation. When the people of a nation honor and protect and provide for their parents, that gives a stability to society which will insure its continuation. When the people of a nation dishonor and discard their parents, this reflects a spirit which will eventually destroy that society.

Children are to honor their parents (that is the inward attitude) and they are to obey their parents (that is the outward action). They are to do this for three reasons: this is what pleases God; this is the right thing to do; and this attitude will create a stable society.

The Challenge to Parents (6:4)

What Paul said up to this point was not unusual in the ancient world. In every society and in every culture, children were expected to obey and to honor their parents. Paul's unique statement on the parent-child relationship is found in verse 4 where Paul said parents have responsibilities, too. Children have responsibilities toward their parents. No one would deny that. The idea that parents also have responsibilities toward their children was new. What are these responsibilities parents have to their children? Paul issued three challenges.

Encourage (6:4)

Paul expressed this challenge in a negative way. Parents are not to "provoke their children to anger." The word "provoke" *(parorgizete)* means to exasperate or to incite. It means to so limit or restrict our children that they are frustrated. A positive way of expressing Paul's challenge is to say, "Fathers, encourage your children. Stimulate them." (Compare Col. 3:1.)

One of the primary personality characteristics of our day is the absence of a feeling of self-worth. This lack of self-worth exhibits itself in several ways. Sometimes it manifests itself by an insatiable desire to dominate. Some people are so insecure they always have to be in charge. This is their way of bolstering a weak ego. Sometimes it manifests itself in depression. I worked with a minister of music one time who had a poor self-image. I would have to pump him up every day because he was always in the dumps. Sometimes it reveals itself in braggadocio. I have a friend who hits me with a long list of what he has done every time we get together. He is trying to cover a poor self-image with a declaration of how great he is.

What do you think is the root cause of all of this poor self-esteem? I believe it goes back to the way we were treated as children. So much of what we do as parents tears down our children's self-image. As Christian parents, we should not provoke our children. Instead, we need to find ways to communicate to our children they are worth something, not because of what they do, not because of what they achieve, not even because of the way they act, but because of who they are, children of God, created in God's image, given to us as a gift. Paul challenged parents not to frustrate or discourage children but to encourage them and help them to realize the potential God has placed within them.

Discipline (6:4)

Paul urged Christian parents to "bring them up in the discipline." "Bring them up" *(ektrephete)* means to nourish or to bring up to maturity. The word translated "discipline" *(paideia)* means to train by ways of commands.

Heated debate surrounds the issue of discipline today. A dignitary from another country said, after a visit to America, "Everything in the American home is controlled by switches—except the children." One mother suggested to her husband, "We need to send the dog to camp and the kids to obedience school!" Evangelist Grady Wilson once said, "Mother had an old razor strap which hung on a nail in the kitchen under a sign that said, 'I need thee every hour.' " Others seem to suggest by their approach to parenting that no discipline is necessary.

The message of God's Word is that discipline for our children is necessary and good, when extended with the right motive. The method of discipline varies with each child. The severity of the discipline is determined by the incident. However, in every case and while using every form, the purpose of discipline is to nourish our child or bring the child to maturity. The responsibility of Christian parents is to help a child realize his fullest potential. Discipline is one of the methods to accomplish this goal.

Instruct (6:4)

The word "instruction" (*nouthesia*) means to train by way of words. The way to bring our children to maturity is by setting guidelines, and then by enforcing these guidelines not only by discipline but also with words of correction.

An important insight on this challenge to instruct our children is found in Deuteronomy 6:7. Two words are used to spell out the nature of parental education: "teach" and "talk." The word "teach" refers to formal, structured times of instruction. These times should be structured into our family life so our children can receive the instructions they need for life. The word "talk" is the informal situational type of communication. This, too, is an important part of our children's education. This happens as we ride along in the car, as we face an emergency, as we play with our children, as we put them to bed. Both in this formal way and in this informal way we must give our children the necessary instruction for them to become all God wants them to be.[3] We accomplish this by teaching them the guidelines which will help them do that.

Conclusion

Two women met at a party after a separation of many years. After the normal greetings, the first woman noticed her friend was wearing an extraordinary diamond ring. She could not help commenting, "That is the biggest, most beautiful diamond I've ever seen."

"Yes," her friend replied, "This is an unusual diamond. It is the Calahan Diamond, and it comes complete with the Calahan curse."

"What is the Calahan curse?" the first woman wanted to know.

The woman with the ring responded, "Mr. Calahan!"

To keep from being the curse our children, parents, or spouse have to put up with, we need to demonstrate our Christian faith in our homes.

For Discussion

1. What are some characteristics of a Christian wife?
2. How can a husband demonstrate his love for his wife?
3. Do children obey and honor their parents today? If not, why not?
4. How does honoring our parents result in longer life?
5. Is discipline necessary in the home? How is this discipline to be administered?

12 | Being a Christian at Work

Ephesians 6:5-9

Dressed in a cap and gown on graduation day, a young man handed his diploma to his father and said, "I've finished law school to please you and Mom. Now, I'm going to be a fireman like I've been wanting since I was six." Many people today are unhappy about the work they do.

A Princeton, New Jersey, psychologist, Dr. Herbert M. Greenberg, has done a revealing study in this field. Based on interviews with more than 250,000 employees of 4,000 firms including every job category and educational group from every part of the country, Dr. Greenberg concluded that 80 percent of all workers at all levels are unhappy and frustrated.[1] Those figures may be inflated. Nevertheless, they indicate a trend toward dissatisfaction at work.

A similar picture is painted in the reports on work in *The Day America Told the Truth*. Reports from the workplace indicate a lack of commitment. Only one in four give their best effort at work. Most admit to spending about 20 percent of their time at work goofing off. Almost half of American workers admit to calling in sick when they are not sick. As the writer concludes, "The so-called Protestant ethic is long gone from today's American workplace."[2]

What is the source of this dissatisfaction?

Compensation.—Some of the dissatisfaction at work relates to our compensation. One man returned home with this sad news for his wife: "Honey, it finally happened. My withholdings this week exceeded my salary!" Not having enough money to provide for our family often creates frustration on the job.

Stress.—Another source of dissatisfaction at work is the pressure of the job. A man who went into business for himself was asked if owning his own business made him independent. "Yes," he responded. "Now, I can arrive at work anytime I like before seven a.m. and I can leave whenever I want after ten p.m." Stress touches workers at all levels. A cartoon showed a cleaning lady, sitting in the chair of the chief executive officer

before he arrived. The caption read, "It's lonely at the bottom, too."
Stress often creates frustration on the job.

Relationships.—One man was fired from his job. When asked why, he
responded, "I was standing around talking and everyone thought I was
the foreman." Relationships between management and labor, relationships between men and women, relationships between older workers and
newcomers—all of these add to the discomfort level at work.

Ross West, in his helpful book *How to Be Happier in the Job You
Sometimes Can't Stand*, lists several elements at work which create
stress: too much work to do, work we are not equipped or skilled to do,
confusion about our role, too many rules and regulations, the impact of
personal life on work life, and the pressure of making decisions.[3]

In a day of growing dissatisfaction, we need a word about how we as
Christians are to relate to our work. Paul's word in our text about how
slaves and masters relate is instructive for us as Christian workers. Notice Paul did not opt for outright emancipation of slaves and destruction
of the institution of slavery at this point. Timing is important for such a
major social change. He did suggest that Christian slaves replace lazi-
ness, ill will, and dishonesty with industry, service, and integrity, and
that Christian masters replace cruelty and selfishness with kindness and
compassion. Such a change in the attitudes and actions of slaves and
masters would eventually transform the system of slavery.

Paul's discussion of masters and slaves can be applied to our relationships at work. We can exchange employees for slaves and employers for
masters, and catch the sense of this passage. This passage could be called
the gospel for the Christian worker.

Remember the overall context of this passage. In chapter 4, Paul explained we have been made new creatures in Christ. This newness is to be
seen in every aspect and every relationship of our lives. Paul applied this
truth to the husband-wife relationship (5:22-33). He applied this truth to
the parent-child relationship (6:1-4). Then, he applied this truth to the
employer-employee relationship (vv. 5-9). Our Christian faith should affect the way we do our work. As one man put it, "Relating one's faith to
one's work is like playing a Christian hymn in a minor key . . . it has a
different sound, but you can recognize it."[4] A Christian should be Christian at work. What does that mean?

The Method (6:5-7)

A Christian's faith should be demonstrated by how he does his work.
Shoddy workmanship by a Christian reflects unfavorably on his faith.

The Christian is to display a different method at work from those who do not know Christ.

A Christian Works Conscientiously (6:5)

How is a Christian to discharge his duties in the workplace? Paul offered three suggestions.

Seriousness of intent.—A Christian is to discharge his duties "with fear and trembling" (v. 5). Paul used the same phrase in two other places. In Philippians 2:12, Paul said we are to work out our salvation "with fear and trembling." Paul told the Corinthians he came to them the first time "in fear and much trembling" (1 Cor. 2:3). To do our work with fear and trembling means to discharge our duties with an anxious care not to come up short, not to do less than what is expected, not to do less than what will call forth praise from our boss.

Singleness of purpose.—A Christian is also to discharge his duties "in the sincerity of your heart" (6:5). The word *sincerity (aploteti)* carries with it the idea of singleness of purpose. That is, we are not only to do our work with an anxious care not to come up short. We are also to carry out our work with an undivided mind, with singleness of purpose.

Sincerity of motive.—In addition, a Christian is to discharge his duties "as to Christ" (v. 5). Everything we do ought to be of such quality that we are not ashamed to show it to Jesus Christ Himself. A modern-day Christian who has displayed this sincerity in his work is Elton Trueblood. His philosophy, to use to the fullest all the gifts God has given us, is summarized in one statement he often made: "Deliberate mediocrity is a heresy and a sin."[5] Because of who God is, we should be driven by a desire to carry out every task conscientiously.

One employer attached a note to the paycheck of a certain employee which said, "Your salary will become effective as soon as you do." That should never be said about the Christian worker. We are to do our work conscientiously with an anxious care not to come up short, with a singleness of mind, so the final product is good enough to show to God.

A Christian Works Consistently (6:6)

A Christian is not only to do his best. He is also to do his best all the time. A Christian is to discharge his duties "not by way of eye service, as men-pleasers, but as slaves of Christ, doing the will of God from the heart."

One of the best illustrations of Paul's suggestion was a television commercial for some brand of after-shave lotion a few years ago. The scene was an office full of workers, who were all busy. One lady was busy filing her nails. Another was busy reading the paper. Another was busy drinking coffee. They were all busy doing nothing! Just before the boss entered the office, they would erupt into action so when he walked through the door they were hard at work. The boss would scratch his head and say, "I don't understand. They always look busy, but they never get any work done." A confidant informs him the scent of his after-shave lotion always reaches the room before he does. The next day, the boss sneaks up on his workers, scentless, and catches them all goofing off.

A Christian is not to work just when he is being watched. A Christian is not to work just when he wants to impress the boss. The Christian, in the final analysis, is not working for his boss but for the Lord. Whether or not our boss sees us, the Lord sees us. Therefore, at all times, whether the boss is there or not, we are to do our best. We are to work consistently.

Few Americans have worked any more consistently than Thomas A. Edison. Although he had a handicap with his hearing, he nevertheless lived a productive life, mainly because of his commitment to work. His workplace was his favorite place to be, and he worked there with a vengeance. Edison filed a patent every two weeks of his adult life. When an explosion shook the film finishing house at the West Orange factory, Edison immediately went to the site. He was seen, directing the firemen and at the same time jotting down notes in one of his small pocketbooks on how to rebuild the factory. His biographer reports that when Edison reached his seventies, he was persuaded to cut down his working day to sixteen hours! From the beginning of his life until his death, Edison consistently did his best at work.[6]

A Christian Works Contentedly (6:7)

The Christian not only does his best. He not only does his best all the time. He also does his best all the time with the right spirit, joyfully and not grudgingly. A Christian is to discharge his duties, Paul said, "with good will, . . . as to the Lord, and not to men."

A traveler in the Tennessee hills stopped to watch a farmer holding a pig in his arms so the animal could eat apples right off the tree. "Won't it take a long time to fatten the pig that way?" asked the stranger. "Sure it will," replied the farmer, "but what is time to a hog?" That man had developed the right attitude toward his work.

The greatest witness we can give at work as Christian employees is not just to do our work but to do our work with such a joyful spirit that others can see the Spirit of Christ in us. When they realize our faith even affects the attitude with which we do our work, they are going to recognize something different in our lives, and we can explain to them the difference Christ makes.

Someone has distinguished three categories of people on any job: the shirkers, the jerkers, and the workers. The shirkers always manage to slip out of their work load. They never do anything. The jerkers jump around a lot and talk their job and make a lot of noise. However, when the dust finally settles, we discover they really did not do much work. The workers roll up their sleeves and get with it. They do their job conscientiously, consistently, and contentedly.

The Motive (6:8)

Why should the Christian do His work conscientiously, consistently, and contentedly? Notice the two motives Paul identified.

Our Responsibility

The first motive has already been expressed in each of the preceding verses. We do our work "as to Christ" (v. 5). We do our work as" slaves of Christ" (v. 6). We do our work "as to the Lord" (v. 7). The reason we are to do our work conscientiously, consistently, and contentedly is that we are doing our work for the Lord. As Christians, we do everything for Him. Therefore, we want to do everything the best we can, at all times, with the right spirit.

Christian businessman Jack Eckerd explained in his autobiography the decision to take soft-core pornographic magazines out of his store. Shortly after his conversion, Eckerd visited one of his stores and noticed the magazine racks. He had never seen them in this light before. On the shelves of his store were a number of magazines featuring nudity. He called the company CEO and asked him to take the magazines out. The CEO explained how much money this would cost the company, but Eckerd insisted. A few days later these unacceptable magazines were removed from the bookracks of all 1,700 Eckerd stores. Someone asked Eckerd if his newfound Christian faith was the reason for this action. "Of course," Eckerd replied, "Why else would I throw a few million dollars out the window?" He concluded with a statement which revealed his motivation: "The reason was simple: the Lord wouldn't let me off the hook."[7]

As Christians, we have a responsibility to do our work in such a way that is pleasing to our Lord. The desire to please Him is the primary motive of Christians in the marketplace.

Our Reward

Paul said we are to do our work conscientiously, consistently, and contentedly, "knowing that whatever good thing each one does, this he will receive back from the Lord, whether slave or free" (v. 8). Let me explain what Paul said in a simple sentence. No good deed is ever done in vain. The good deeds we do have a way of coming back to us. It might not be immediately, but eventually it will happen. Jesus said, "But when you give alms, do not let your left hand know what your right hand is doing, that your alms may be in secret, and your Father who sees in secret will repay you" (Matt. 6:3-4). If not in this life, the Bible is clear our good deeds will come back to the Christian in the life to come. Jesus told the disciples, "And everyone who has left houses or brothers or sisters or father or mother or children or farms for My name's sake, shall receive many times as much, and shall inherit eternal life" (19:29).

Christian commitment cannot be capsuled in the "spiritual" dimension of our life. Instead, our commitment to Christ spreads to every aspect, every dimension, every task, and every relationship. Thus, our Christian faith will not only be displayed in the method of our work but also in the motive of our work.

The Mandate (6:9)

Not many Christians were slave owners and masters in Paul's day. Nevertheless, Paul had a word for them in verse 9: "And masters, do the same things to them, and give up threatening, knowing that both their Master and yours is in heaven, and there is no partiality with Him."

The radical element in what Paul said about Christians at work was his mandate to the managers. He followed the same pattern here as in his word about the husband-wife relationship and about the parent-child relationship. In the relationship between husbands and wives, Paul started with the responsibilities of the wives because that was commonly accepted. But then he went on to say, "Husbands have responsibilities, too." In the relationship between parents and children, Paul started with the responsibilities of the children because that was commonly accepted. But then he went on to say, "Parents have responsibilities, too." Likewise, in the relationship between masters and slaves, Paul started with the responsibilities of the slaves because that was commonly accepted. But then he went on to say, "Masters have responsibilities, too." What are the responsibilities of masters or bosses? Again, Paul focused on both method and motive.

The Method

How were Christian masters to relate to Christian slaves? Paul told the masters to "do the same things to them" (v. 9). About whom is Paul speaking? This is a reference to the employees or slaves. He told employees to do their best, all the time, with the right attitude. He challenged bosses to do the same thing. Bosses are to do their best toward their employees, at all times, with the right attitude. That's the positive expression of the responsibility of Christian bosses.

Paul expressed the truth negatively in the next phrase: "and give up threatening them." The word for "give up" *(anientes)* means to loosen up or to relax. Paul told the Christian masters to lighten up, to relax, to quit trying to intimidate their slaves. So, Paul told the masters to relate to their slaves with understanding and patience.

Harry Gordon Selfridge, management expert in London, distinguished between two types of executives: leaders and bosses. He said, "The boss drives the people; the leader coaches them. The boss depends upon authority; the leader, on goodwill. The boss says, 'I'; the leader, 'We.' The boss fixes the blame for the breakdown; the leader fixes the breakdown. The boss knows how it is done; the leader shows how. The boss says, 'Go!'; the leader, 'Let's go!' "8 Using that terminology, we can say: Christian executives are to be leaders, not bosses. They are not to lead by intimidation and manipulation but by encouragement and example.

The Motive

Why should they do this? The motivation is found in the last part of verse 9: "knowing that both their Master and yours is in heaven, and there is no partiality with Him." The Lord does not provide more privileges for certain people than he does for some others. The Lord does not consider some people to be more important than others. Therefore, the boss is to treat his workers with the same kind of understanding, patience, and concern he expects from the workers.

A frequently told story describes an editor of a newspaper who for fifty years had been successful in his journalistic career. As a reward for his hard labor, the owner of the newspaper urged the editor to take a six-month-vacation with full pay. The editor considered the offer and then refused for two reasons. "The first reason," he said, "is that if I quit writing my column for six months it might affect the circulation of your newspapers. The second reason is that it might not affect the circulation!"

Whether or not our presence at work affects the bottom line is not the primary question for a Christian employer or employee. The key question is: does my work make a difference for Christ? For we are to be Christians even at work.

For Discussion

1. Why are so many people dissatisfied with their work?
2. Why should the Christian worker be conscientious about his work?
3. What is our motive for doing our work well?
4. What can we do to increase the enjoyment of our jobs?
5. Is it possible to be a Christian at work? What are the hindrances?

13 | Going to War for God

Ephesians 6:10-24

A little prospector, wearing clean new shoes, walked into a saloon in the days of the old West. A big Texan said to his friend standing at the bar, "Watch me make this dude dance." He walked over to the little guy and said, "You're a foreigner, aren't you? From the East?"

"You might say that," the newcomer responded, "I'm from Boston and I'm here to find some gold."

"Tell me something," the Texas returned, "Can you dance?"

"No, Sir," came the reply, "I never did learn to dance."

"Then, I'm going to teach you. You'll be surprised how quickly you can learn." With that the Texan took his gun and started shooting at the prospector's feet. Hopping, skipping, and jumping, the little prospector somehow made it out of the saloon. The Texan and his friends had a big laugh.

About an hour later, the Texan left the place. As soon as he stepped outside the door, he heard a click. He looked around and, four inches from his head, was the biggest shotgun barrel he had even seen. Holding the shotgun was that little Bostonian who said, "Mr. Texan, have you ever kissed a mule?"

All of us have enemies, people who do not like us, people who create problems for us. As Christians, we have an enemy. Life for the Christian is not a leisurely stroll. It is a battle against the principalities and powers. In these closing verses of his Ephesian Letter, Paul showed how we can be prepared for spiritual warfare.

Know Our Enemy (6:10-13)

All the way through, the Bible talks about the power of evil at work in the world. In Luke 10:18, the enemy is called "Satan." In Matthew 4:1, the enemy is called "the devil." In John 12:31, he is referred to as "the prince of this world"(KJV). In Matthew 4:3, he is spoken of as "the tempter." In 2 Corinthians 4:4, he is singled out as "the god of this world." All of these references are to our enemy, Satan.

117

Much mystery surrounds this evil character known as Satan. Mystery surrounds his origin. In Genesis 1—2, the Bible describes God's creation of the world and gives this conclusion, "It was good." Suddenly, in Genesis 3, Satan appears in the form of a serpent. Where did he come from? We do not know. Mystery also surrounds his fall. Satan apparently was an angel who somehow fell out of favor with God. How and why? The Bible does not specifically answer this question, although some see an allusion to the fall of Satan in Isaiah 14:12-15.

Mystery shrouds our perception of Satan. However, one thing is absolutely clear. About one thing there is no uncertainty or mystery at all. The devil stands in opposition to God. His purpose is to destroy the works of God. His purpose is to discourage the people of God. His purpose is to discredit the word of God. His purpose is to oppose everything good and godly in the world. He is the enemy of every Christian. Paul described our enemy in our text.

He Is Strong

Satan is not to be underestimated, for he has tremendous power to use against the Christian. Satan is so strong, the only way we can oppose him is in the strength of God's might (v. 10). Satan is so tough, only by putting on the full armor of God will we be able to stand against him (v. 11). The struggle with Satan is not to be compared to a struggle with flesh and blood but a struggle against rulers and powers and world forces of darkness (v. 12). Everything Paul said implies Satan is a strong enemy with whom we have to contend.

An old wag suggests: "Don't invite the devil to get in the car with you. Pretty soon, he will want to drive!" That's good advice. I have seen some who are too caught up with and too obsessed with the devil. More common is the tendency to think Satan is inconsequential. To quote the book title, *Satan Is Alive and Well on Planet Earth.* He is at work and he is our enemy. He opposes everything we do and his opposition is strong.

He Is Subtle

In verse 11, Paul referred to "the schemes of the devil." The Greek word *methodeias* is the source of our word *methods.* We need to watch out for the methods of the devil. What does that mean? It means Satan is not going to come dressed with a pitchfork, red uniform, pointed ears, and a long tail. Satan is not going to come to us dressed up in something evil looking or unappealing so we can say, "That's Satan. I'd better watch out for him." That is not the way he works. As he came to Eve in the beginning, so he will come to us, dressed in an attractive, appealing, interesting disguise in order to gain our approval before we ever realize who he is. We need to watch out for him. He is tricky. He is sneaky. He will come up behind us when we least expect him. He is subtle.

He Is Sinister

Paul referred to Satan as "the evil one" (v. 16). Peter, in his First Epistle, said Satan wants to devour our life (1 Pet. 5:8). Jesus described Satan as a "murderer. . . . a liar, and the father of lies" (John 8:44). Make no mistake about it. Satan is not weak. He is strong. He is not obvious in his methods. He is subtle. He is not a nice friend to associate with. He is like a lion who is trying to devour our lives.

Satan is not as "mere" as we have thought him to be. He is strong, subtle, and sinister. He is the archenemy of the Christian. Because he is strong, we need to stay close to the Lord. Because he is subtle, we need to keep our eyes open. Because he is sinister, we need to be aware of his motives. That is why Jesus warned His disciples, "Keep watching and praying, that you may not enter into temptation. The spirit is willing, but the flesh is weak" (Matt. 26:41). We have an enemy who is opposed to us.

Know Our Equipment (6:14-17)

How are we going to face this enemy? How are we going to deal with one who wants to destroy the work of God, discredit the Word of God, and discourage the people of God? We need to wear the right equipment.

Several years ago I watched a special video called "Fights of the National Football League." This eight-minute film showed some of the fights which erupted during professional football games. One sequence showed a player on the sideline. A fight breaks out on the field, so this player rushes toward the action. Suddenly, he stops and runs back to the sideline. He puts on his helmet, and then dashes back into the midst of the fist-swinging players. He wanted to be prepared for battle!

As Christians, we need to be prepared for battle against our archenemy Satan. God provides the protective equipment we need to fight the battle. Paul urged the Ephesians to "put on the full armor of God" (v. 11). Then he described this armor.

The Belt of Truth (6:14)

To prepare for battle, the first step is "girding your loins with truth." Paul had in mind the belt the Roman soldier used around his waist. He wore a long, flowing robe. Whenever it was time to run or whenever it was time to fight, he would take the robe and tuck it up under his belt or

girdle so he could fight and run without getting tripped up in his skirt.
"Girding your loins" was the prelude to battle or flight. The belt or girdle
held everything together for the Roman soldier.

Truth holds everything together for the Christian. How do we prepare
to face our enemy and live as the new persons that Jesus Christ made us
to be? We gird everything together with the truth. In our dealings with
others, we commit ourselves to honesty. In our relationship with our
family, we commit ourselves to honesty. In making our decisions about
life, we commit ourselves to honesty. When we commit ourselves to the
truth, when we live by the truth, then we have something that holds us
together as we fight our enemy.

The Breastplate of Righteousness (6:14)

The second piece of equipment is the "breastplate of righteousness."
The breastplate was the piece of equipment covering the vital part of the
body. It would protect against the fiery darts and the arrows aimed for
the heart. When the enemy shot the fiery darts or arrows toward a person's chest, the breastplate repelled them and, thus, protected the person.

The breastplate for the Christian is righteousness. A negative and positive application can be made. Nothing will so destroy our influence, our
joy, our peace, our power, and our victory as will unrighteousness. When
we yield to temptation, we allow Satan to obtain a foothold in our life. To
allow unconfessed sin to remain in our life, to let unrighteousness remain
in our life, gives Satan a foothold against us. On the other side of the coin,
one of the things that repels Satan, that keeps him from having an effect
on our lives, is an unswerving commitment to righteousness. When we
live righteously before the Lord, Satan can do nothing to us.

The Sandals of Readiness (6:15)

To prepare for battle against Satan, Paul challenged the Christian to
have "shod your feet with the preparation of the gospel of peace." Some
translations say, "put on the sandals of readiness." Sandals are the equipment to which Paul referred. Readiness is the quality Paul had in mind.
In the Roman world, sandals were not loose-fitting flip-flops. They con-
sisted of a piece of leather with knobs underneath, almost like spikes.
Strings of leather were brought from the leather base over the instep and
around the legs three or four times. These sandals were an essential part
of their equipment because they gave the soldier his footing and enabled
him to stand firm when fighting against his enemy.

We Christians must be clothed with a spiritual awareness and mental
alertness which will enable us, at any given moment, to strike a blow

against the enemy and for Christ. Abraham Lincoln once said, "I'll prepare, and someday my chance will come." To have that kind of attitude toward our spiritual life is to put on the sandals of readiness.

The Shield of Faith (6:16)

To prepare for spiritual battle we must also take up "the shield of faith with which you will be able to extinguish all of the flaming missiles of the evil one." The shield is the equipment and faith is the quality. What did Paul mean by the "shield of faith?" He was talking about trust. There are two kinds of faith. There is the "if" kind of faith. "If" You will bless me, Lord, and "if" You will give me good things, and "if" You will make Your face to shine upon me, then I will serve You. That's the "if" kind of faith. Even if You don't bless me, and even if You don't give good things to me, and even if You don't make Your face shine upon me, "nevertheless," still, I will trust You. That's the kind of faith Paul had in mind.

It is the faith of Shadrach, Meshach, and Abednego, the three Israelites who refused to bow down to the idol. The king said, "If you don't do it, I'm going to throw you into this furnace." They said, "Our God is able to deliver." That's what we remember. But we often forget what they said next. They went on to say, "And even if He doesn't, still, we will serve Him" (Dan. 3:17-18, author's paraphrase). That's the kind of faith Paul had in mind.

Preparation for spiritual battle is preceded by a decision to put our life in God's hands and leave it there, regardless. Unswerving commitment and trust in the Lord are shields that ward off the fiery darts of the evil one.

The Helmet of Salvation (6:17)

What is "the helmet of salvation"? Paul was not talking about the experience of salvation but the power which comes to those who are saved. When we are saved, we have the Holy Spirit living within us who provides power to face the challenges of life. This power available through the Spirit will help us win the victory and oppose the enemy. This power comes to us in the heat of the battle. As we stand for the truth, as we live a righteous life, as we prepare ourselves spiritually to serve God, and then launch out with confidence in God, we will experience a power which will enable us to face any enemy and win the victory.

The Sword of the Spirit (6:17)

Paul identified the "sword of the Spirit" as "the word of God." That is a major piece of our equipment as we fight the battle against the evil one.

When we love the Word of God, read it, study it, learn it, meditate upon it, apply it to our life, it will become like a sword with which we can oppose our enemy.

With the sword of the Spirit, we can go into spiritual battle. As long as we live, Satan is going to attempt to undermine our influence and to rob us of our joy. He has already done that for some of us. By planting certain thoughts in our mind, by getting us involved in certain things, by leading us to respond to certain temptations, he has already robbed us of our joy. Like David, we need to come back and say, "Lord, restore unto me the joy of thy salvation." We need to do that every day, all the way through our Christian life. We will never come to the place where we can say, "I have it made now. He's not going to bother me anymore." The Christian life is not a playground. It is a battleground. That's why we need the sword of the Spirit.

With the sword of the Spirit, we can win the victory. If we will make a commitment to the truth, if we will dare to live in righteousness, if we will be prepared each day to serve the Lord when those opportunities come, if we will trust Him and put our lives in His hands, if we will daily yield to the power which is available to us, if we will spend time every day in the Word of God and hide His Word in our hearts—if we will do all of those things, then we can win the victory over Satan. For that is the equipment which will prepare us to engage in spiritual warfare.

Know Our Empowerment (6:18-20)

In addition to the equipment God provides for us, we Christians have an energy produced within us. This energy is released within us through the practice of prayer. Paul began his Letter to the Ephesians by reminding them of his constant prayers of their behalf (1:15-16). He ended the letter by requesting them to pray constantly on his behalf (6:19). In this challenge Paul declared some important truths about prayer.

What? (6:18)

Paul explained first of all what to pray. We are to pray "with all prayer and petition." The word *proseuches* is the general word for *prayer* and is preceded by the modifier *all*. Some people just pray one kind of prayer. They are always asking God for something. That's what prayer is for them. Like the little boy whose mother asked him if he said his prayers before he went to bed. "No," the little boy said, "I didn't need anything tonight." Paul challenged us to pray with all prayer which would include praise and thanksgiving and confession as well as petition.

The word "petition" *(deeseos)* is a specific word which implies the request for specific needs. We are not just to be general in our prayer like the man who prayed, "God bless everyone everywhere." We are to become aware of specific situations and specific needs and take those to the Lord in prayer.

What are we to pray?—prayers that include thanksgiving, praise, confession, and intercession, which also present specific petitions for specific needs. We are to pray with variety and with specificity.

When? (6:18)

Paul also explained when to pray. We are to pray "at all times" (v. 18). Some people just pray in emergency situations. The only word God ever hears from them is *help.* In a certain school, a sign on the wall said, "In case of an earthquake, the ban against prayer will be temporarily discontinued." That is the idea many of us have of prayer. We pray in emergency situations.

In contrast, Paul said we are to pray at all times. We are to pray, when things are going well and when things are not going well. We are to pray, when the sun is shining and when we are caught in the storms. Prayer is to be a constant practice in the life of the Christian. As Paul put it in another place, we are to pray without ceasing (see 1 Thess. 5:17).

Where? (6:18)

Then Paul told us where to pray. We are to pray "in the Spirit" (*v.* 18). Literally, this means we can pray anywhere, with the Spirit's help. We can pray anywhere, when we are in harmony with His will. We do not have to be at church to pray. We do not have to be in our home to pray. We can pray at work. We can pray as we drive our car (although if we do this, we need to follow the biblical admonition "watch and pray"). Where are we to pray? We can pray anywhere as long as we are in the Spirit.

How? (6:18)

In addition, Paul taught us how to pray. We are to "be on the alert with all perseverance and petition" (v. 18). What does that mean?

With awareness.—We are to "be on the alert." The Greek word *agrupnountes* means to be attentive or vigilant. It means to be aware as over against sleepy. It implies an awareness of the problems around us and an awareness of the promises of God's Word so we can pray intelligently for the application of God's promises to those problems.

With persistence.—We are to continue in our prayers. The word *"perseverance" (proskarteresei)* means to give constant attention. In other words, we are to look around and see the problems that need to be addressed. Then, we are to look into God's Word and see the promises that apply to the problems. Then, we are to pray and pray and pray until an answer comes. We are to pray with awareness and persistence.

For Whom? (6:18)

Paul also revealed for whom we are to pray. We are to pray "for all the saints" (v. 18). Not just the ones we like. Not just the ones who pray for us. Not just the ones who support us and encourage us. We are to pray for all the saints.

Paul went from a description of prayer to a request to pray specifically for him. Notice how different Paul's desire for himself is from our desires for ourselves. When we ask others to pray for us, we usually want them to pray for release from some situation. We want them to pray for personal safety or personal comfort. Paul did not pray for release from his situation but for the power to use that situation to further the gospel. He did not pray for personal safety or personal comfort but for spiritual power.

When we ask others to pray for us, our interest is usually for ourselves. Paul's interest was for the spread of the gospel. Paul was a prisoner in Rome. He faced possible death. Yet, he did not pray for release or for safety. In effect, he prayed for two things. He prayed that when he opened his mouth he would have a message from God. And he prayed that when the opportunity arose, he would have courage to open his mouth. He prayed for spiritual energy to enable him to win the victory for Christ.

Conclusion (6:21-24)

Paul concluded his Letter to the Ephesians with a summary of the abundance which can be ours as Christians. This abundance can be summarized in three words: *peace, love,* and *grace.*

Peace (6:23)

Paul wanted the Ephesians to experience peace. What is peace? It is a sense of inner security in the midst of whatever experiences life throws at us. How can we have that peace? Jesus cut to the heart of the issue in His statement in John 16:33: "These things I have spoken to you, that in Me you may have peace. In the world you have tribulation, but take courage; I have overcome the world."

Peace does not come from outward circumstances. Jesus clearly promised we would have problems in the world. Our circumstances are never perfect. Life is never easy, even for the Christian. We can still have peace, however, because our peace does not come from outward circumstances. It comes from inner confidence, not that God will deliver us from our problems but that God will deliver us through our problems.

Some people bear three kinds of trouble: all they ever had, all they have now, and all they ever expect to have! Christians do not have to live like that. We can have the peace which comes from Jesus Christ.

Love (6:23)

Paul wanted the Ephesians to experience "love with faith." What does that mean? It means the kind of love for the brethren which grows out of our faith in and trust toward God. Loving others is tough. As the anonymous poet put it:

> To dwell there above
> With those we love,
> That will be glory.
> But to dwell here below
> With those we know,
> That's another story!

How can we love the unlovely? Where does this love come from? John touched the core of the issue in his beautiful statement in his First Epistle: "We love, because He first loved us" (1 John 4:19). Love is not something we have to conjure up from within us. Love is something which grows out of our relationship with God. As we draw close to God, His love flows through us to others.

Christian love stands in contrast to the world's love. The world's love focuses on self and asks the question, "What can you do for me?" Christian love focuses on the other person and asks, "What can I do for you?" This Christian love grows out of our faith and trust in God.

Grace (6:24)

Paul also wanted the Ephesians to experience God's grace. The word *grace* is a synonym for all the riches of God. It is another word for "every spiritual blessing" (1:3) which Paul promised the Christian at the beginning of this epistle. Thus, Paul began and ended this epistle of abundance by reminding the Christians at Ephesus that God wanted to fill their lives full.

Harold Kushner related a saying from the Talmud. According to this saying, "In the world to come, each of us will be called to account for all the good things God put on earth which we refused to enjoy."[1]

The great tragedy in the church today is that we often refuse to allow God to be as good to us as He really wants to be. We go through life in spiritual poverty when He wants us to be rich. We go through life empty when He wants us to be full. God surrounds us with good things He wants us to enjoy, but we refuse to claim them for our own. That's why we need to hear again the fantastic promises of Ephesians. If we will open ourselves to the spiritual blessings our Heavenly Father has made available to us, then we can begin *Living Abundantly.*

For Discussion

1. What do we need to remember about Satan?

2. Which piece of spiritual equipment described by Paul is most important. Why?

3. How does righteousness protect us in spiritual battle?

4. What is the difference between an "if" kind of faith and a "nevertheless" kind of faith?

5. How can we begin to experience more of the abundance Christ has available for us?

Notes

Chapter 1

1. Mamie McCullough, *Get It Together and Remember Where You Put It* (Dallas: Word, 1990), 159-60.
2. William Barclay, *The Letters to the Galatians and Ephesians* (Philadelphia: The Westminster Press, 1954), 89.
3. Barclay, 96.
4. Warren Wiersbe, *Be Rich* (Wheaton, IL: Victor Books, 1976), 23.

Chapter 2

1. Stuart Briscoe, *Let's Get Moving* (Glendale, CA: Regal Books, 1978), 25.
2. Richard J. Foster, *Celebration of Discipline* (San Francisco: Harper, 1978), 31.
3. John F. MacArthur, Jr. *Keys to Spiritual Growth* (Old Tappan, NJ: Fleming H. Revell Company, 1976), 78.
4. Barclay, 102-03.
5. Wiersbe, 30.

Chapter 3

1. E. Stanley Jones, *A Song of Ascents* (Nashville: Abingdon Press, 1968), 16.
2. Ray Summers, *Ephesians: Pattern for Christian Living* (Nashville: Broadman, 1960), 36.
3. Mary Ann O'Roark, "Marlo Thomas: My Life Gets Better All the Time," *McCalls*, August, 1978, 89.
4. Virginia Douglas Dawson and Betty Douglas Wilson, *The Shape of Sunday* (Houghton Mifflin Co., 1952), 51.

Chapter 4

1. Quoted in Leslie B. Flynn, *Come Alive with Illustrations* (Grand Rapids: Baker Book House, 1988), 52.
2. William Hendriksen, *Galatians and Ephesians* (Grand Rapids: Baker Book House, 1968), 130.
3. Barclay, 131.
4. Ibid., 136.
5. Ibid., 138.

Chapter 5

1. Malcolm Forbes, *Women Who Made a Difference* (New York: Simon and Schuster, 1990), 290-293.
2. Quoted in Bryan Jay Cannon, *Celebrate Yourself* (Waco: Word, 1977), 90.
3. Jack B. North, "Traveling Light," in *Pulpit Digest*, March-April, 1982, 44.
4. Hendriksen, 155.
5. Stephen Brown, *No More Mr. Nice Guy* (Nashville: Thomas Nelson, 1986), 101.
6. Max Lucado, *The Applause of Heaven* (Dallas: Word, 1990), 79.
7. James P. Wesberry, *Evangelistic Sermons* (Nashville: Broadman, 1973), 22.
8. Charlie Shedd, *How to Develop a Praying Church* (Nashville: Abingdon, 1964), 37.

Chapter 6

1. Barclay, 155-56.
2. Bill Blackburn, *What Should You Know About Suicide?* (Waco: Word, 1982), 115-16.
3. Joe Griffith, *Speaker's Library of Business Stories, Anecdotes and Humor* (Englewood Cliffs, NJ: Prentice Hall, 1990), 269.

Chapter 7

1. Barclay, pp. 161-62.
2. Hendriksen, 192.

Chapter 8

1. George Barna, *The Frog in the Kettle* (Ventura, CA: Regal Books, 1990), 33-38.
2. Tony Campolo, *Wake Up, America* (Harper: San Francisco, 1991), xi-xii.
3. Paul Powell, *The Great Deceiver* (Nashville: Broadman, 1988), 34.
4. James E. Hightower, Compiler, *Illustrating the Gospel of Matthew* (Nashville: Broadman, 1982), 24-25.
5. Jack Gulledge, editorial in *Proclaim*, October-December, 1979, 3.
6. *The Minister's Manual, 1981* (San Francisco: Harper and Row, 1981), 249.
7. Daniel Okrent and Steve Wulf, *Baseball Anecdotes* (New York: Harper and Row, 1989), 108-09.

Chapter 9

1. Forbes, 110-13.
2. *Time*, May 9, 1983, 82.
3. *Quote*, Vol. 75, 325.
4. Michael Duduit, *Joy in Ministry* (Grand Rapids: Baker Book House, 1989), 46.

Chapter 10

1. Barclay, 194.
2. John R. W. Stott, *Baptism and Fullness of the Holy Spirit* (Downers Grove: InterVarsity, 1976), 60-61.
3. Luther Joe Thompson, *Through Discipline to Joy* (Nashville: Broadman, 1966), 46.
4. *Albuquerque Journal*, October 8, 1991, A3.

Chapter 11

1. Summers, 118.
2. Hendriksen, 248.
3. Howard Hendricks, *Say It with Love* (Wheaton, IL: Victor Books, 1972), 95.

Chapter 12

1. Nelson Price, *Supreme Happiness* (Nashville: Broadman, 1979), 41-42.
2. James Patterson and Peter Kim, *The Day America Told the Truth* (New York: Prentice Hall, 1991), 155.
3. Ross West, *How to Be Happier in the Job You Sometimes Can't Stand* (Nashville: Broadman, 1990), 80-86.
4. J. Emmett Henderson, "Christian Ideals and Economic Realities," *Pulpit Digest*, September-October, 1976, 6.
5. James R. Newby, *Elton Trueblood: Believer, Teacher, and Friend* (New York: Harper and Row, 1990), 162.
6. Ronald W. Clark, *Edison: The Man Who Made the Future* (New York: G. P. Putnam's Sons, 1977), 7, 214, 231.
7. Jack Eckerd and Charles Conn, *Eckerd: Finding the Right Prescription* (Old Tappan, NJ: Fleming H. Revell, 1987), 189.
8. Griffith, 192.

Chapter 13

1. Harold Kushner, *When All You've Ever Wanted Isn't Enough* (New York: Pocket Books, 1986), 82.